AIRFIX
magazine guide 28

The English Civil War

George Gush and Martin Windrow

Patrick Stephens Ltd
in association with Airfix Products Ltd

First published— 1978

ISBN 0 85059 259 3

Cover design by Tim McPhee

Text set in 8 on 9 pt Univers Medium
by Stevenage Printing Limited,
Stevenage.
Printed in Great Britain on Fineblade
cartridge 90 gsm and bound by the
Garden City Press, Letchworth,
Herts.
Published by Patrick Stephens
Limited, Bar Hill, Cambridge, CB3 8EL,
in association with Airfix Products
Limited, London SW18.

Don't forget these other Airfix Magazine Guides!

Contents

Acknowledgements

Unless otherwise credited, all photographs are the authors'. Abbreviations used in credits: DOE—Department of the Environment, Crown Copyright Reserved; NAM—National Army Museum, London.

Editor's introduction

The English Civil War marked the end of an era in British history, so it is appropriate that it should form the subject matter of this book, the last in our series of *Airfix Magazine Guides*. George Gush, a history lecturer and author of *Renaissance Armies 1480-1650*, has made a serious study of the period over several years, with the result that this book is probably the most accurate concise introduction to the period currently available. Covering the origins of the conflict, the course of the war and its major battles, and the organisation and weapons in use, his lucid text will be useful to anyone beginning a study of the English Civil War as well as providing detailed background information for wargamers. George, of course, is also a wargamer of no small stature, and author of the Wargame Research Group's Rules for the English Civil War period. Thus, in addition to the historical information, he has also included an account of a game designed to show how these rules work in practice.

It is unfortunate that Airfix do not, as yet, produce any OO/HO scale English Civil War figures suitable for wargamers, but they do, of course, make three superb 54 mm figure kits in their Collectors' Series. In the second part of this book, co-author Martin Windrow describes how to add extra authenticity to these models, and convert them into alternative poses. The figures were actually made by Gerry Embleton, but they were painted one weekend by yours truly—so don't blame Gerry for the results! In addition to the practical modelling information, however, Martin also provides useful background information on basic styles of dress during the English Civil War.

Apart from the model and wargaming photos, all the illustrations in this book come from contemporary documents or depict preserved weapons and items of equipment in museums, so their authenticity is guaranteed. The final product is a handy introduction to a fascinating period of history which is rapidly 'catching on' amongst modellers and wargamers.

The book is also, as I mentioned above, the last projected title in our series of *Airfix Magazine Guides*. All good things, it is said, must come to an end, and we have come a long way since Gerald Scarborough wrote the first title in the series (*Plastic Modelling*) in 1974. The subject matter of the books in the series have ranged from practical military, aircraft and naval modelling titles to detailed monographs on aircraft, camouflage and markings, tanks and various aspects of military history, plus four—or, with this, five—popular titles for wargamers. We at Patrick Stephens Ltd are always receptive to ideas for good books, so if there is some title which you would have liked to have seen in this series, and which could be developed into a good book, do drop us a line. In any case, whether this is the first or the twenty-eighth *Guide* you have bought, thank you for your support.

BRUCE QUARRIE

one

The English Civil War

Although there were three English Civil Wars between 1642 and 1650 (and these should really be called 'British', since both kingdoms were involved), the second and third were essentially only postscripts to the Great Civil War with which we are here concerned, starting when Charles I raised his standard at Nottingham in August 1642, and ending with his surrender in the spring of 1646.

Although we are concerned with the military aspects of the war rather than the politics, we must at least attempt to say, first, what it was about. This is no easy task. It has been seen as a religious conflict between Puritans and Anglicans, a constitutional one between Divine Right and the rights of Parliament, a Marxist struggle of bourgeoisie against feudalism, or a battle of interests between court and country, 'ins' and 'outs', a result of Stuart incompetence or Parliamentary ambition, of the rise of the gentry, or the decline of the gentry, or goodness knows what else.

Perhaps it would be fair to say that the King saw himself as defending his rightful and traditional powers and prerogatives, and the traditional discipline of the Church of England, while his opponents felt they were defending equally traditional individual rights and Parliamentary privileges, and 'True Religion'. The King's 11 years of personal rule had created fears of despotism, and resentments over favouritism, inefficiency, restraints upon enterprise and weakness in foreign affairs, and the outbreak of Catholic rebellion in Ireland perhaps provided the final spark, arousing all sorts of hatreds and fears and creating a fatal and final confrontation over control of the army which would now need to be raised.

However this may be, the war certainly settled many things—chief among them the ultimate sovereignty of Parliament, and its echoes can, not unfairly, be heard to ring through subsequent divisions of English society—Anglican and nonconformist, Whig and Tory. Its repercussions and ideas led indirectly to the American and French Revolutions of the next century, and its impact on its own time was immense—the execution of the King rocking monarchical Europe, the grim efficiency of Cromwell's England fore-shadowing Empire to come.

The social and political background of the struggle affected military events in many ways, giving the war its special character.

Firstly, it was being fought in a country which, partly because of financial weakness of the Crown, had no armed forces apart from the militia. Their armouries and sketchy training formed a minimal basis, only the well-equipped Trained Bands of London and the brave Cornishmen showing any real effectiveness. Thanks to the Thirty Years' War and the Eighty Years' War of Holland and Spain, there was a fair smattering of officers with military experience. But many others, like most of the men in the ranks, had to learn their new trade as they went along, perhaps with the dubious aid of one of the now-numerous military training books (most of which revelled in formations and evolutions of incredible complexity and uselessness, calculated, one would suppose, to tie any untrained body of pike and shot into an inextricable knot!).

Officers and men included, at one extreme, religio-political enthusiasts such as Cromwell recruited into his Ironsides—men who knew what they fought for (it might not coincide closely with what their leaders in Parliament believed the cause to be) and fought with more than a touch of fanaticism. Others were loyal to cause or King, but might have doubts about the war. The

Parliamentary commanders Essex and Manchester were of this stamp, a fact which certainly affected events. Then there were great numbers whose loyalties were primarily local or personal, like those tenants of Lord Derby who went with Rupert to Marston Moor, the hard-fighting Cornishmen, or the King's standard-bearer, Sir Edmund Verney, whose sympathies lay with Parliament, but who had served the King too long 'to desert him now'. At the other extreme, there were many with little or no interest in, or understanding of, the conflict — levies and conscripts, village no-goods swept up by the armies and so on; or 'pure' professionals, like the Scot, Sir John Urry, holder of the Civil War all-comers' side-changing record. Such troops, according to the common practice of the day, could readily be enrolled in their captor's forces when made prisoner (a point to be considered when wargaming in this period). There were some foreign mercenaries too, one splendid example being the Croat, Carlo Fantom, who thus summed-up *his* interest: 'I care not for your Cause; I come to fight for your halfe-crownes and your handsome woemen' (a useful officer, especially as, John Aubrey tells us, he was magically bullet-proof — anyone called Captain Phantom obviously ought to be! He served first the Earl of Essex, then the Royalists, coming to a bad end when they hanged him at Oxford 'for Ravishing', a hobby which his previous employers, rather surprisingly, seem to have taken less seriously). Rupert claimed to have captured French, Irish, Dutch and Walloons, and there were even some Americans — returned New Englanders in the forces of the Eastern Association.

Otherwise, the war was very much confined to Britain; only the King had any real hope of assistance from other nations — Holland, Denmark and Portugal were the possibilities — and as, ironically, Parliament controlled the fleet created by his hated Ship-Money, as well as most of the ports, there was little chance of its reaching him (although, through the Queen, he *was* able to pawn the Crown Jewels and buy some arms abroad).

The other possible external influence was Ireland, where the King hoped, firstly, to recall English troops fighting the Catholics; and secondly, to gain aid from the Catholic Confederates. The first was achieved after his representative, the Earl of Ormonde, signed a truce or Cecession in summer 1643. The second was a harebrained scheme which came to nothing, but probably did more than anything else to discredit his cause, as the average Englishman of the day hated only one thing worse than a Papist, and that was an Irish Papist. In fact, Parliamentary propagandists managed to persuade their countrymen that even the *English* troops from Ireland were Irish Papists too!

With little influence from outside, then, the political and physical geography of Britain would dictate the general pattern of the war.

Probably a majority of the population deplored the war and sought to avoid involvement in it. Though they were liable to suffer looting (not much), billeting of troops, heavy and illegal taxation and even impressment, many in that age of small population and slow travel could remain fairly isolated from events, though few could match the blissful ignorance of the labourer of Long Marston who, when asked in the *third* year of the war which he was for, King or Parliament, asked 'What, be they two fallen out, then?' Happy man. By 1644 some positive resistance to the war had developed, with crudely-armed 'clubmen' defending their property against both sides (although sometimes co-operating temporarily with one or the other).

Many, though, *were* involved, and there was some sort of roughly discernible pattern of loyalties. Presbyterians and Independents in religion for Parliament, High Anglicans and the few Catholics for the King, who also had the support of a majority of the Peers, the greatest landowners. The ports, the manufacturing towns, London and the south-east were predominantly Parliamentarian, the more rural and traditional areas of the west, Wales and the north more strongly Royalist.

This gave some shape to the struggle.

The English Civil War

The King, who had abandoned London and raised his standard at Nottingham, needed for both political and economic reasons to regain his capital, but it proved very difficult to concentrate his scattered and peripheral forces for this object.

Parliament, on the other hand, was extremely vague as to objective, and to begin with had half-hearted commanders, but held many of the trump cards: most of the richest and most taxable areas, most taxable trade, most areas useful for making munitions (London, Birmingham and Kent and Sussex, although Charles held the Forest of Dean, Cornish tin and Welsh lead) and most of the main Royal Armouries—the Tower, Hull and Portsmouth. What is more, although the Committee of Public Safety was much less effective at *military* direction than the King's Council (itself a pretty quarrelsome body), it proved much better on the financial and administrative side.

Thus the Royalists would be generally on the offensive, with the initial advantages of a good deal of ready cash, plate and so on from the King's aristocratic supporters; cavalry much superior to Parliament's makeshift horse; and a single Commander-in-Chief in the person of the King himself (quite a good commander but liable to trust the bad judgement of others rather than rely on his own sound views). As time passed, however, the advantages of their opponents would become increasingly important. If Charles did not win the war quickly, he would become less and less likely to win it at all.

However, the very nature of the war made rapid victory difficult to achieve. The sides were pretty evenly matched. Moreover, the simple pattern mentioned was subject to innumerable exceptions; Royalists in Kent and the City of London, plenty of Parliamentarians in north and west; everywhere communities, neighbours and even families divided, and numerous local and personal quarrels adding their force to the general struggle—and in a civil war local control was vital for recruitment and finance. Thus a great part of the strength of both sides had to be dissipated in garrisons, and much more was swallowed up in purely local and small-scale campaigning. It was necessary, but even if it hadn't been, local magnates and locally raised forces would have been unwilling to go far afield and were primarily interested in local enemies. The summary which follows sketches some of the main movements, but they should be understood as taking place alongside an infinitely complex background of minor actions which cannot be detailed here, but had much effect on the main operations. Because of this, field armies tended to be small, often assembled for particular operations and dispersed again afterwards in a way that would have had von Clausewitz chewing the study carpet in sheer frustration. Principles like maintenance of aim and concentration were strikingly absent from the planning of both sides— usually half a dozen objectives were pursued at once, which at least kept the jealous and quarrelsome generals apart. And although many commanders— notably Prince Rupert and Cromwell— were much more willing to accept the test of battle than were their mercenary contemporaries of the Thirty Years' War, victories in the field tended to prove indecisive; the defeated recruiting their strength from garrisons, the winners dissipating theirs. Thus the decisive success which Charles needed was likely to elude him.

two

The course of the war

1642

The main campaign was that of Edgehill. The King's army, aiming for London, detoured to collect men from Wales and money from Oxford; the Earl of Essex, with Parliament's main force, needing to secure the valuable Severn Valley, allowed the King to get between him and London, but met him at Edgehill. After the battle, the King's slow advance secured Oxford (his capital for the rest of the war) and Reading (commanding westward communications from London) but allowed Essex to get back and, with the Trained Bands, stop him in a bloodless confrontation at Turnham Green.

Significant events elsewhere included the securing of Hull and Portsmouth for Parliament; fighting in the north favoured the Royalists, but in the west they were strongest only in Cornwall. By the end of the year Parliament had improved its organisation by forming associations of counties (the Eastern Association the best known), and there were some peace talks, and proposals from the Scots for alliance with the King, or mediation. None came to anything, partly because the King expected to win next year.

Battles

Powick Bridge, September 23: Significant only as first real action of the war. Prince Rupert, the King's nephew, with eight troops of horse and ten companies of dragoons, defeated ten troops of horse and five companies of dragoons of Essex's advance guard, inflicting 150 casualties.

Edgehill, October 23: The King's army (10,500 foot, 4,000 horse and 20 guns) descended the steep Edgehill to fight Essex's force (slightly weaker in cavalry, but stronger in foot). On both wings the Royalist horse, charging at the gallop, broke the Parliamentarians but pursued too far and mostly returned too late to affect the stubborn infantry fight in which some Parliamentary horse were involved and of which the Royalists had slightly the worse. Losses about 1,500 a side, the Royalists also taking seven guns; both sides withdrew.

Tadcaster, December 6: Main encounter in the north. Lord Fairfax, Parliamentary leader in Yorkshire, holding Tadcaster with 1,500 men, beat off the Earl of Newcastle, Royalist leader in the north, with 4,000, inflicting 100 casualties. 2,000 Royalist horse and dragoons supposed to be marching on the enemy rear failed to appear.

1643

This year saw the high water mark of the Royalist cause and depression on the part of Parliament, with only narrow defeat for the peace party. Sir Ralph Hopton's string of victories secured the west for the King; the great port of Bristol was taken; Newcastle's forces dominated the north-east, while in the north-west troops from Ireland began to arrive, building up Lord Byron's Royalist army.

In the centre, an incursion by Waller to Royalist Wales was defeated in spring, and for a time a triple-pronged advance against the Parliamentary south-east seemed possible, but it was not really seriously planned, and failed to materialise. Newcastle, who moved as far south as Lincolnshire, could possibly have overrun the Eastern Association, especially as Kings Lynn had declared for the Royalists, but he turned back to besiege Hull instead, unsuccessfully. Hopton's Cornishmen could not be brought to leave the west, especially with Plymouth still untaken, and although a new-formed force under his command advanced as far as Sussex, it then spread out in winter quarters, allowing Waller to retake Alton, Romsey and Arundel. The King

The English Civil War

Newcastle

York
Marston Moor
Tadcaster   Hull
Adwalton
Moor

Gainsborough

Rowton   Lincoln
Heath   Winceby
Chester
  Nantwich   Newark

Hopton   Nottingham   Kings Lynn
Heath

Leicester

Naseby

Worcester
Powicke   Edgehill
  Bridge   Cropredy Bridge
Hereford
Ripple
Gloucester   Field   Stow

OXFORD
Chalgrove
Field
LONDON

Bristol   Roundway
Down   Reading
Lansdown   Devizes   Newbury
Basing   Farnham
Ho.

Langport   Cheriton

Taunton
Arundel
Stratton
Exeter   Portsmouth
Sourton
Down
Lostwithiel   Plymouth
Fowey

himself, rejecting suggestions for a march on London, turned to reduce Gloucester, whose gallant defence seemed to give new hope to the flagging Parliamentary cause. Essex made a skilful march to its relief, and the King's last chance of decisive victory this year fled when he failed, at Newbury, to destroy Essex's returning army.

Battles

Bradock Down, January 19: Royalist forces which had retired into Cornwall, with the local militia, under Hopton and

Nearly 5,000 of the King's horse and foot drawn up at the end of the 1639 Bishops' War. This shows a fairly typical battle array, although the guard out in front, the musketeers behind their pikes, and the harnessed up artillery show the army is on parade or moving (NAM).

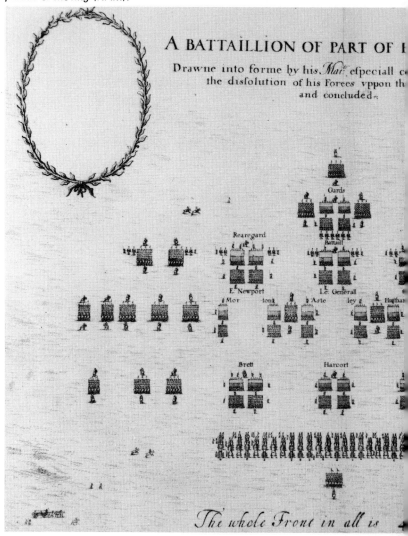

The English Civil War

Sir Bevil Grenvile, defeated an equal Parliamentary force under Ruthin, who lost nearly 1,500 prisoners and four guns.

Hopton Heath, March 19: Battle near Stafford, resulting from Royalist attempts to regain Lichfield. Sir John Gell and Sir William Brereton, with about 1,500 men and three heavy and eight light guns, were attacked by about 1,200 under the Earl of Northampton

(killed during the battle). Royalist charges drove off the Parliamentary horse and repeatedly overran their guns; they retreated during the night, losing their guns and about 500 men to the Royalists' 50.

Ripple Moor, April 13: Sir William Waller, with 1,500 horse and a few foot and guns, attacked Prince Maurice (Rupert's younger brother) with 2,000 foot, near Tewksbury. His attack was repulsed and his army scattered by a Royalist attack as it withdrew, losing about 80 casualties.

Sourton Down, April 25: A check, in Devon, to the advance of Hopton's army (3,000 foot, 300 horse, 300 dragoons and four guns). After driving back James Chudleigh's force (1,500 musketeers, 200 pikemen and five troops of horse), Hopton was ambushed in the dark and forced to retreat.

Stratton, May 16: Hopton, with 2,400 mainly Cornish foot and 500 horse, attacked Stamford's 5,400 foot, 200 horse and 13 guns in a strong position at Stamford Hill, near Stratton, Cornwall. Four converging columns took the hill, killing 300 and taking 1,700 prisoners, 13 guns, a mortar, and supplies.

Chalgrove Field, June 18: Rupert, with 1,000 horse, 500 commanded foot and 350 dragoons, was intercepted in the Oxford area when returning from an attempt on a pay-convoy betrayed by Urry, by a stronger force which he routed by cavalry charges, John Hampden, MP, being killed.

Adwalton Moor, June 30: Newcastle, with 10,000 men, was attacked on a ridge near Bradford by Lord Fairfax with 4,000 trained troops and some ill-armed irregulars. Although enclosures allowed the Roundheads to stem Royalist charges, a final attack by pikemen under Colonel Skirton broke into their left, leading to a near collapse of their army with 500 killed and 1,400 men and three guns taken.

Lansdown, June 5: Men brought by Prince Maurice and Lord Hertford raised Hopton's army to 4,000 foot, 2,000 horse, 300 dragoons and 16 guns. Sir William Waller, sent to stop him, held a strong position on Lansdown hill. Three Cornish attacks, secured the hill

The course of the war

after very heavy losses, but before Waller retired he had fought the Royalists almost to a draw, scattering their horse. Sir Bevil Grenvile killed.

Roundway Down, July 13: Hopton, shaken by injuries from a powder explosion, was besieged with 3,000 foot at Devizes by Waller, who had made up his army to 2,500 foot, 2,000 horse and eight guns. Prince Maurice and the horse went to Oxford and brought back Lord Wilmot with 1,800 cavalry and two galloper guns; this force broke Waller's cavalry wings, while many of his infantry surrendered when the Devizes garrison belatedly came up. Waller's army lost all guns, ammunition and baggage, 600 killed, 800 taken, and the rest dispersed.

Bristol, July 23-26: Nathaniel Fiennes, with 1,500 foot, 300 horse and nearly 100 guns to hold three miles of defences, capitulated after Rupert's troops broke into outer defences. Fall of many other towns in the west quickly followed.

Gainsborough, July 28: Cromwell and Meldrum, with 20 troops of horse and four companies of dragoons (circa 1,200 men), defeated Cavendish, besieging Gainsborough with 30 troops of horse and dragoons from Newcastle's army. Success in this cavalry battle due to Cromwell's retention of a reserve.

First Battle of Newbury, September 20: Essex, with 10,000 foot (half from London Trained Bands) and 4,000 horse, found the King's army (8,000 foot, 6,000 horse and 20 guns) across his road to London. Royalist inertia allowed him to take a good position on high ground, and Royalist attacks brought on a rather confused fight in awkward terrain. Artillery played a large part, and the Royalist horse did well, the foot, apparently, poorly. A draw would have favoured the King, but shortage of ammunition caused his withdrawal, allowing Essex to resume his march.

Winceby, October 11: 1,500 Eastern Association horse defeated Sir William Widdrington with 1,500 horse and 800 dragoons. Cromwell drove back 1st line; Sir Thomas Fairfax's flank move with Parliamentary 2nd line broke Royalists. Another Parliamentary cavalry victory.

1644

The King had narrowly missed victory in 1643 because of localism, because of Parliament's command of the sea, which enabled it to support Hull and Plymouth, because of Gloucester's gallant resistance, and perhaps finally through his own refusal to make concessions to the moderates among his enemies. The last service of Pym, the dying Parliamentary leader, had been to conclude the Solemn League and Covenant with the Presbyterian Scots, and January 1644 saw over 20,000 men under the Earl of Leven take the snowy road to England—and with them, Charles' star began to set. Indeed, the disasters that 1644 brought to the Royalist cause are less surprising than its survival and resilience, mostly attributable to divided and faulty military and political leadership on the other side.

After early defeats at Nantwich in the north-west, Cheriton in the west (the first major victory for Parliament) and a success at Newark, the Royalists planned to concentrate on the north where Newcastle, at York, was besieged, eventually by the Scots, the Northern army of the Fairfaxes, and the Eastern Association army under Manchester. Rupert regained Lancashire, relieved Lathom House and successfully raised the siege of York, but then met disaster at Marston Moor, costing the King an army and the north.

Naturally, the Royalists failed to pursue a *single* objective, but also reinforced their western armies, while in the centre the King decided not to stay on the defensive as planned, a more active policy involving the abandonment of Reading to create a field army. Manchester refused to move against him, but Waller and Essex did so, soon threatening Oxford and chasing the King to Worcester (leading him to pen a desperate letter to Rupert which led to the battle at Marston Moor). However, he was saved by Essex's departure to the west and his own partial victory over Waller at Cropredy Bridge, and proceeded to follow Essex west to win an astonishing success at Lostwithiel. Though confronted by Waller and

The English Civil War

Manchester at Newbury on his return, Charles was able to avoid disaster and relieve vital garrisons.

By the year's end, despite the loss of the north, where the Scots were besieging Newcastle and the Fairfaxes mopping up Yorkshire, the King and his advisers were remarkably confident, partly because of Presbyterian-Independent disputes and other disagreements between their enemies, partly because of news from Scotland. Here, after the breakdown of a grand plan for invasion and uprising, the Marquis of Montrose, almost alone, had evaded the covenanters to link up with a small Scots-Irish invasion force led by the giant warrior Alastair MacDonald. With this and varying numbers of Highlanders, Montrose started an extraordinary campaign, winning two sweeping victories before the end of the year.

Although the Moderates entered into talks with the King at Uxbridge, Parliament was taking steps which would put paid to Royalist hopes — the Self-Denying Ordinance of December, which would get rid of half-hearted generals, and the New Model Army (not finally formed till next spring), a properly equipped and paid *national* army at the disposal of the Committee of Both Kingdoms for use anywhere in the country.

Battles

Nantwich, January 25: Lord Byron, besieging the last Parliamentary stronghold in the north-west with 1,800 horse and 5,000 foot, was caught with his army divided by the River Weaver, by Sir Thomas Fairfax and Sir William Brereton, with 1,800 horse, 500 dragoons, 2,500 foot and several hundred ill-armed 'cudgellers'. His cavalry were held off while his foot were destroyed by a central breakthrough, losing 1,500 men, their guns, baggage and most of their colours.

Relief of Newark, March 22: Newark, held by 1,500 foot and 300 horse, controlled north-south routes. Rupert, with 6,400 men, defeated Sir John Meldrum's besieging army (2,000 horse, 5,000 foot, 11 guns and two mortars), scattering the horse in a surprise onset, then trapping the foot. Parliament lost 200 killed, 3,000 muskets, all guns and baggage. Newark secured for two years more.

Cheriton, March 29: Hopton and Lord Forth, with 2,200 horse, 3,000 foot and 12 guns, defeated by Waller with 3,000 horse, 7,000 foot (including two London Trained Band regiments) and 17 guns, losing 300 killed to his 60. After 1,000 Royalist musketeers drove a similar force from Cheriton Wood, an advance post threatening their left, the Royalists intended to stand, but were drawn into an attack on their right which eventually involved all their cavalry, and were defeated by artillery, a narrow lane, and Haselrig's Lobsters. Meanwhile, Waller attacked their left and they were forced back to their start-line, subsequently withdrawing.

Cropredy Bridge, June 29: Waller (5,000 horse, 4,000 foot, 11 guns and two battery guns) was marching parallel with the King's army of 5,000 horse and 3,500 foot, on opposite banks of the Cherwell, north of Banbury. Crossing the river to attack the Royalist vanguard, which had become separated, Waller was cut off by Lord Cleveland's horse and had to fight his way back with the loss of his guns and about 700 men (many deserted) to the Royalists' 14 killed and 70 taken.

Marston Moor, July 2: Rupert outmanoeuvred the Allied besiegers who awaited him west of York, and reached the city. Next day he caught the Allies withdrawing south at Marston Moor, but the late arrival of the foot from York allowed them to return and deploy on a ridge. After a long wait, a general attack took the Royalists by surprise. Goring's Northern horse on their left defeated those of Sir Thomas Fairfax, and many Scots infantry joined the rout, disaster being avoided by the stand of Lord Lindsay's brigade. On the other flank, Cromwell and David Leslie scattered Rupert's horse after a hard fight, moved across the field and defeated the remnants of Goring's men, and finally assisted the foot to destroy the Royalist infantry, fighting continuing into dark-

The course of the war

ness with the stand of Newcastle's White-coats in an enclosure. The largest battle of the war: the Allied army of about 7,000 horse, 20,000 foot and 30 or more guns losing 300-1,000 dead, the Royalist force of at least 6,500 horse, 11,000 foot and 20 guns losing 3,000-3,500 killed, all their guns, and practically all their foot taken or scattered.

Lostwithiel, August 21-September 2: The King, with 16,000 men, followed Essex's 8,000 foot and 2,000 horse into the west and trapped them on the coast at Lostwithiel. Royalist attacks started on the 21st, when they took and fortified Beacon Hill. The Parliamentary horse subsequently escaped through the thin 16-mile cordon. The retreat of the foot to Fowey was hotly pressed by the King and after a battle at Castle Dore (August 31), Essex escaped by sea, Skippon surrendering 42 guns, 5,000 muskets and 6,000 prisoners (who were released).

Tippemuir, September 1: Montrose, with 3,000 ill-armed foot, defeated Lord Elcho's 6,000 foot, 800 horse and seven guns. Montrose's men, deployed only three-deep, charged with a single volley just when the repulse of a skirmishing force disarrayed the Covenanters, who broke, losing 2,000 dead to the Royalist single man, as well as 1,000 prisoners. As in most of the Montrose's battles a long pursuit accounted for most of the casualties.

Aberdeen, September 13: Montrose, with 1,500 foot, 80 horse and seven guns against 2,500 foot, 500 horse and some guns. After driving off piecemeal cavalry attacks and a flanking move, a mass charge broke the Covenant infantry on their ridge, killing 1,000 for a loss of 12.

Second Battle of Newbury, October 26-27: The King's 9,000 men faced a combined force of Waller's, Essex's and Manchester's troops, plus the London Trained Bands, about 17,500 in all. Manchester fought the Royalists frontally, while Waller with over half the Parliamentary army made a long flank march to attack the Royalist left under Prince Maurice. Despite fierce fighting,

the flank attack did not break through, nor did Manchester's belated frontal attack. Losses about 500 a side.

Fyvie Castle, October 28: A two-day defensive success for Montrose's 800 foot and 80 horse, against the Duke of Argyll with 2,500 foot and 1,200 cavalry.

1645-1646

The Royalists were now reduced to the Chester - Oxford - South Wales-Bristol-Devon-Cornwall area, and even here the forces of the Northern Association threatened Byron at Chester, while those of the Western

The English Civil War

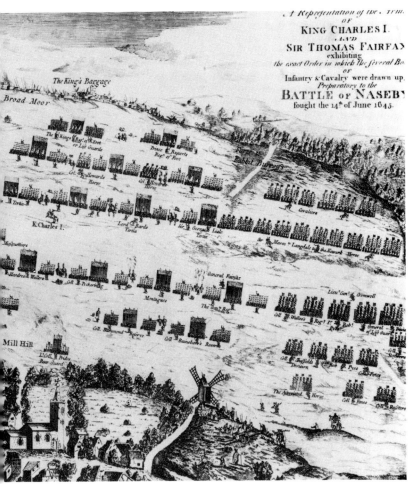

Engraving of the battle of Naseby, 1645, made just after the first Civil War. Though probably somewhat distorted by the artist, this gives a good idea of the deployment of armies during the Civil War (NAM).

Association challenged the Royalist hold in Wales. Elsewhere they had only isolated garrisons, and they were racked with quarrels centering on the rivalry of Rupert and Lord Digby. Nevertheless they remained at first remarkably hopeful, encouraged by Montrose's continued success, which stimulated more than one northward march by the King's army and also reduced the effectiveness of Leven's Scots force in England (although it still managed to reduce several strongholds and got as far south as Hereford). What was more, Goring with the Western army advanced as far as Farnham in the spring, alarming London and provoking a counter-raid by a cavalry force under Waller. However, Parliament's hold on points such as Taunton and Plymouth, and quarrels between the King's western leaders, prevented any really effective Royalist moves from this direction.

The course of the war

Parliament at first directed Sir Thomas Fairfax and the New Model to this area, to raise Goring's siege of Taunton, but diverted him to Oxford when it was learnt that the King was moving north.

To draw him away from that under-provisioned city, the King's army captured Leicester on May 29. Sir Thomas, given, for the first time, a free hand, came unexpectedly upon the Royal army which, perhaps unwisely, decided it would have to fight. Detachments to garrison Leicester and other places had reduced the army to a strength' which made the disaster at Naseby almost inevitable.

With this defeat, the end was clearly in sight, as Royalist strongholds were gradually reduced and individuals began to make their peace with Parliament (as Rupert urged the King to do). In July the only remaining field army was shattered at Langport, and September saw three critical blows. First, Rupert surrendered Bristol, saving his 1,500 men, but not their arms and being temporarily sacked from command as a result. Secondly, the defeat of part of the King's forces at Rowton Heath left Chester to an inevitable, although not immediate, fate. Last, and worst, Montrose after gaining control of Scotland with Kilsyth, saw his Highland and Irish followers disperse traditionally about their own business, leaving his move toward England to end in utter disaster at Philiphaugh. Gallant Basing House fell in October, when a last effort to send aid to Montrose also failed, and by early 1646 it was a question of mopping-up.

The defeat of the King's last western force at Torrington made inevitable the surrender of Exeter and the other Royal garrisons there. At Stow on the Wold, 3,000 foot, virtually the last field troops, capitulated.

'You have done your work, boys, and may go play, unless you will fall out among yourselves', the brave Lord Astley told his captors, and a couple of weeks later, on May 5, the King surrendered to the Scots army. He still hoped to profit by the division of his enemies, but the Scots sold him to Parliament for £400,000 (much of which, it is pleasant to note, they never received), and his further efforts in this direction led him to the block. Although the war was really over, Oxford held out until June 24, and the last Royalist stronghold, Harlech, until March 16 1647!

Battles

Inverlochy, February 2: Montrose's 1,500 men, with one troop of horse, made a circuitous mountain march in terrible weather to surprise Sir Duncan Campbell's 1,100 regular infantry and 2,000 Campbell clansmen. The usual wild charge broke the Covenant line and killed 1,500, including the commander, for a loss of 12.

Auldearn, May 9: Montrose's 2,000 foot and 250 horse fought 4,000 foot (including many veterans) and 600 horse under Sir John Urry—one of two armies threatening Montrose. Sir John was drawn into a frontal attack over difficult ground against Montrose's apparent position on a ridge, and his army was broken when the latter's main body, which had been concealed in a hollow, attacked its right flank. Urry lost his baggage, 16 colours and 3,000 men killed to Montrose's 200.

Alford, June 2: Baillie's Covenanters marched across Montrose's front under the impression that his mainly hidden army was in retreat, and were then attacked, downhill, with their backs to a marsh. The Gordon horse on the Royalist right initiated the fight, and were assisted by Irish swordsmen to defeat their opponents and join in against the centre, which broke with the appearance of Montrose's reserve. Montrose had 2,500 foot and 250 horse; Baillie, with fewer foot but 600 horse, lost 1,600 dead.

Naseby, June 14: Rupert, with at most 4,500 horse and 4,000 foot, made an uphill attack upon Fairfax and the New Model—about 6,500 horse and 7,500 foot. On the Royalist right, Rupert's cavalry defeated Ireton's, but went out of control, as usual. On their left, Langdale's horse were defeated by Cromwell's, who then rallied and attacked the left of the outnumbered

Royalist foot who, remarkably, were making headway against their opponents. The Royalist reserve retired through a mistake when the Earl of Carnwath restrained the King from a counter-attack, and some of Ireton's horse, plus Okey's Dragoons (who had occupied hedges ahead of the Parliamentary left) also joined in against the unhappy Royalist foot. Most were captured after a hard fight, but one brigade resisted to the last. Royalist losses between 400 and 1,000 killed and 4,500 taken, with all guns and baggage.

Langport, July 10: Goring's 7,000 men and two guns were rather recklessly attacked while in a very strong position by Fairfax with 10,000. Owing to difficult terrain only the latter's artillery, some horse, and some commanded musketeers really got into action but, probably because of low morale and discipline in Goring's army, these proved sufficient to defeat him, with 300 Royalists dead and half the rest scattered.

Kilsyth, August 15: Baillie, with 6,000 foot and 800 horse, uphill from Montrose's 4,400 foot and 500 horse, was forced by his accompanying Covenanting Committee to march across Montrose's front to secure another ridge and prevent the Royalists' 'escape'. Montrose's horse defeated the vanguard of this movement; the next units, which had become isolated, were overrun by a highland charge, and a general attack in support destroyed the Covenanters, who lost 6,000 dead to the Royalist six.

Philiphaugh, September 13: Montrose, advancing toward England with a scratch force of one Irish regiment and some recent recruits, 1,500 in all, was surprised near Selkirk by David Leslie with at least 4,000 horse and dragoons from Leven's army. The Irish, deserted, surrendered on terms after half of them had died in a heroic stand. Their Godly opponents afterwards murdered them, and all the women and children who had accompanied the army.

Rowton Heath, September 24: Langdale's 3,000 horse of the King's army, attempting to take the besiegers of Chester in the rear, were defeated by Sydenham Poyntz with 3,500 horse and 300 foot, a sally by the garrison being also thrown back.

Torrington, February 16 1646: Fairfax, with 6,000 foot, 3,500 horse and 500 dragoons, turned a patrol clash into an impromptu night assault on Hopton's 2,000 foot and 3,000 horse, in the town on their way to relieve Exeter. The Royalist force was scattered for a loss of 200.

three

Weapons and equipment

The Foot

The English Civil War was fought at a time when the development of firearms had almost—but not quite—swept away the armour, spears and bows of the Middle Ages.

The weapon which dominated the battlefield was the matchlock musket, the strong points of which gave infantry a central role in warfare, while its weaknesses made it necessary for other weapons to be carried too, and allowed cavalry to remain, to a great extent, the decisive striking force.

Despite a trend toward shorter and lighter muskets, those of the Civil War could have a barrel some four feet long and weigh up to some 16 pounds, and thus normally had to be supported on a forked rest stuck in the ground, while firing (this rest could have a spike or blade at the top, when it was called a 'Swedish Feather' or 'Swinefeather', and could be used as a barrier against cavalry, like archers' stakes in the Middle Ages. Such devices were imported during the Civil War, and seem to have been used by, for example, Hopton's men at Sourton Down). As muskets got lighter, rests tended to be

discarded, but they seem to have been in pretty general use during the Civil War.

A musket would be bored to fit, usually, a lead ball weighing 1/12 lb, though a 1/14 lb ball might be used to speed loading; however, there was not much standardisation, and a musketeer normally carried both a mould to make bullets for his particular gun and 'pruning-iron' for scraping down issued or captured shot to fit!

Like most of the firearms of the next 200 years, the musket was a smooth-bore muzzle-loader, and was fired by a lighted 'match' held in a pivoted arm or 'serpentine' which stubbed into the powder in the firing-pan when released by pulling the trigger. The match was what we would now probably call a fuse, made of cord boiled in vinegar, and was consumed in great quantities by 17th Century armies, every musketeer having to carry a length lighted at both ends when in the presence of the enemy.

Matchlocks were rugged, simple and cheap (in the 1631 'Gunmakers' Rates' a complete musket with bullet mould and worm and scourer for cleaning cost 15s 6d). They could be made or repaired by very ordinary craftsmen, and ammunition, apart from powder, quickly improvised—bed-cords (17th Century equivalent of springs) could be boiled for match, roofing-lead or household pewter melted down and cast into ball. What is more, the musket with its large bullet and long barrel could 'spoyle' an unarmoured man at 30 score paces (500 yards), a man in 'common armour' at 20 score, or in 'musket proof' protection at ten score. Its shortcomings were, for a start, the match, which used itself up, blew out, caused nasty accidents when

Wheel-lock holster pistol of carbine-like appearance, 1635 (DOE).

The English Civil War

Left *An elaborate buff coat, which belonged to Major Thomas Saunders, of Gell's Regiment of Horse.* **Right** *Rear view of the same* (NAM).

excited infantrymen drew fresh powder from the regiment's 'budge barrel' during battle, and tended to give away your position at night (in compensation, it also offered a neat way of convincing the enemy you were still there when you weren't!).

Second, and more serious, the musket was extremely inaccurate; the deep infantry formations of the day made this less serious, but at longer ranges or against 'forlorn hopes' of skirmishers this would much reduce its effect.

Nor could this defect be made up for by a high rate of fire — the third problem, indeed, was the long time taken to reload. Paper cartridges were known but bullet, charge and priming powder were normally carried separately, bullets in a small bag, powder in a flask, charges in 12 cases dangling from a shoulder-belt. As the musketeer opened one of these cases with his teeth, trying not to swallow his mouthful of ready-use bullets, holding his musket in one hand and a couple of feet of match, lighted at both ends in the other, with his four-foot rest slung to one wrist with a loop of cord, muttering to himself the 48 separate movements of loading distinguished by contemporary drill books, we may readily apprehend that, however well-trained and devoted he may have been, he was *not* going to get off more than one shot a minute at best!

Firepower in battle would be further reduced by misfires (Kellie, in *Pallas Armata*, 1627, said that 30 to 40 per cent misfires would not be unusual) — wind or rain could prevent firing altogether — and by smoke; the sulphurous powder of the day creating so much that

English flintlock holster pistol of about 1640, typical of those carried in the Civil War (DOE).

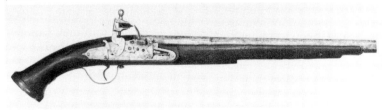

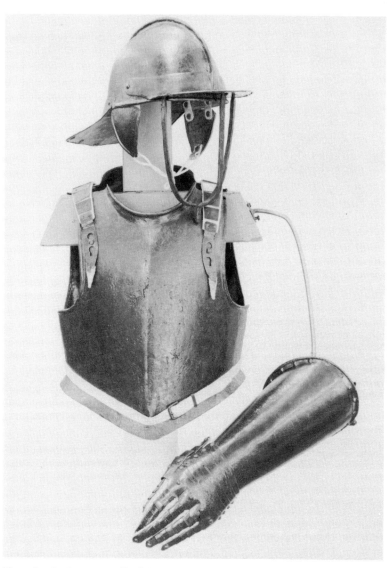

'Arquebusiers' armour—English triple-barred pot, corselet, and gauntlet for bridle arm. Standard Civil War cavalry equipment (DOE).

'getting the wind of the enemy' (ie, upwind) was an important tactical consideration.

The superior flintlock had already been developed, but in the Civil War was confined to horsemen and artillery train guards (lighted matches being too dangerous near all that powder). So had the rifle, offering much greater accuracy, but this only appeared in sporting guise in the hands of ex-keepers and the like, the snipers of the war.

Thus, as Robert Ward (*Animadversions of Warre*, 1639) observed, while

The closed helmet and three-quarter armour of a cuirassier. German, circa 1630 (DOE).

'Shot are the principall members (as the armes are to the body) of an army, if they be wisely and advantagiously plac'd and made use of . . .' yet they were '. . . of themselves too weak to resist the Horse, unless the wisdom of the Generall place them in such places of advantage in which they might secure themselves.' Even if a musketeer opened fire at long range — say 300 yards, as some writers advocated — he could hardly hope to fire more than twice before attacking cavalry were on him, and neither his clubbed musket nor his cheap sword were ideal weapons for a man on foot against a man on a horse.

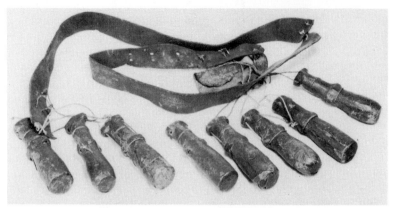

Musketeer's bandolier (NAM).

Various people were busily attempting to invent the bayonet at the time but, until they succeeded, musketeers in the open would require the support of pikemen.

The pike, of course, was no more than a stout 15- to 18-foot spear. Those who carried it were supposed to be the tallest and strongest members of their unit and, unlike the musketeer, to wear armour of the type illustrated—open helmet, corselet, and tassetts for the thighs. Hot, heavy and expensive (£1 2s in 1632), armour was beginning to be discarded, but was still in manufacture and use throughout the Civil War, although many individuals and even units might be unable to obtain it. A thick leather 'buff coat', usually sleeveless and long-skirted, was usually worn under, or sometimes instead of, the armour.

Pikes and muskets were the standard infantry weapons; officers might carry partisans, and sergeants, halberds, but these bladed pole-weapons were too few to have a significant effect on the battlefield (except, of course, to the unfortunate individual who met one!). Newly raised troops often had only improvised weapons—bills, cudgels and the like, while among the Scots (both Covenanters and Royalists) traditional weapons like Lochaber axes and the similar Jedburgh staves were still sometimes used. Highlanders employed longbows, almost vanished in England, and for close-quarter work, round leather-covered shields or 'targes' and claymores—still sometimes very large *two*-handed swords. In each of the London Trained Band Regiments, 50 men were armed with the 'bow-pike', a peculiar combined weapon, but there seems no record of its use in action.

The Horse

The great majority of mounted men were equipped as 'Harquebusiers' or 'Light Horsemen'—misleading terms, since they didn't normally carry an arquebus, and were definitely *heavy* cavalry by the standards of a later day. The basic arms of such a horseman comprised a sword—normally a long

Matchlock musket of about 1640. Note serpentine, with screw for clamping match, and firing pan with swivelling lid (DOE).

The English Civil War

Musketeer's powder-flask (circa 1650) (NAM).

straight cut-and-thrust 'tuck', but rapiers such as 'Pappenheimers' were also carried — and two pistols carried in holsters at the saddlebow. Some Scots apparently had *four* guns, and a fair number of men may have lacked them altogether. These pistols were either flintlocks (the early 'snaphance' variety) or wheellocks, the latter producing a spark in much the same way as a cigarette lighter does, by spinning a serrated wheel against a piece of iron

Musketeer's equipment (DOE).

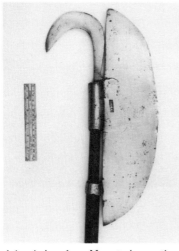

A Lochaber Axe. Mounted on a three-to six-foot shaft. Note the hook, supposed to be useful for hooking men off horses, cutting reins, etc (NAM).

pyrites. They were extremely long (often more like a small carbine than a pistol as we know it) and heavy, being of 20 to 24 bore, and could thus be used as club or missile in close combat. Normally they were smoothbores, with an effective range of a few yards only, but some rifled ones were manufactured during the Civil War, with an unscrewing barrel to allow breech loading, and much greater accuracy and armour-piercing effect.

Although military books usually recommended a carbine or arquebus of 17 to 24 bore, with a barrel up to 30 inches long, carried slung by a swivel from a shoulder-belt, such weapons would appear to have been very rarely carried by Civil War cavalry. Short 'horseman's axes', slung, as the sword could be, by a 'ribbon' from one wrist, were sometimes used, and the Scots had many regiments equipped wholly or in part with light 12-foot lances,

Armour and helmet made for New Model Army Pikemen, circa 1650 (DOE).

17th Century halberd. Six to eight feet long, this was mainly carried by sergeants (NAM).

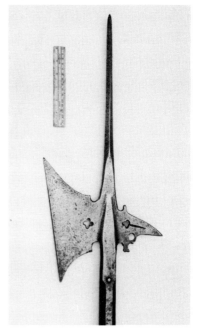

The English Civil War

somewhat antiquated but evidently effective weapons, usually carried in conjunction with a pistol.

Standard wear for the 'light horseman' was the buff coat, gauntlets, cuirass and 'pot' shown, though a good many might lack some or all of the armour, and a steel skull-cap or 'secreit', worn beneath hat or cap, could substitute for the helmet. Mail shirts, or mail sleeves, were still sometimes used, and so were 'jacks' of leather or canvas, with iron plates sewn in — particularly by the Scots lancers.

A few cavalry — individuals and troops, but probably only one full regiment, Haselrig's Parliamentarian 'Lobsters' — wore the cuirassier armour still common in European warfare. Giving almost complete protection as the illustration shows, this equipment had the drawbacks of heat and excessive weight (it was much heavier than a medieval knight's harness, having a musket-proof breastplate and the rest pistol-proof) and cuirassiers were very costly to equip, to mount, and to pay (3s 6d a day to the light horse-

Simple sleeveless buff coat, of the type which might be worn both by horse and foot (NAM).

A 'morter' from Hexham. The gunner's quadrant in the muzzle was used to check elevation (NOT while firing, as here!). Explosive shells can be seen beside the mortar (NAM).

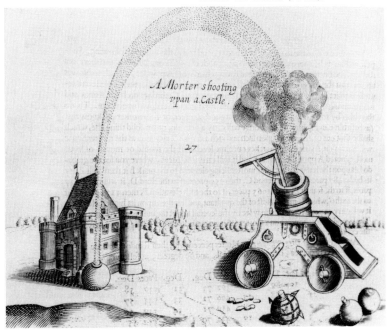

A Morter shooting
vpan a Castle.

27

Sighting (*Hexham*) (NAM).

man's 2s 6d) so, according to Colonel William Barriffe (*Principles of the Art Military*, 1661) 'Some few troops of Curiassiers (sic) were in use at the first, but afterwards reduced, and the Charge saved'.

Dragoons

An invention of the 17th Century, the dragoon of the English Civil War had not yet climbed the social ladder to become a fully fledged cavalryman, but was purely a mounted infantryman on a cheap horse (in the New Model Army, dragoon mounts were half the price of

Chart from one in Ward, 'Animadversions of Warre'.

The names of the pieces of Great Ordnance now in most use	Bore of piece	Diameter of shot (ins)	Weight of shot in pounds	Weight of Serpentine Powder	Weight of Corned Powder*	Weight of piece (lbs)	Length in feet	Length of planks of carriage (feet)
Cannon	8	7 3/6	64	40	32	8,000	12	16¾
Cannon Serpentine	7½	6¾	52	25¼	26	7,000	11½	16¾
French Cannon	7¼	7	46¾	25	23¼	6,500	12	16¾
Demi Cannon Eldest	6¾	6½	36⅝	20¾	20	6,000	11¼	15½
Demi Cannon Ordinary	6½	6¼	32	20	18	5,600	10½	15¾
Demi Cannon	6	5¾	24½	18	16	5,000	11	16
Culverin	5½	5¼	19	16	15	4,500	13¼	18¼
Ordinary Culverin	5¼	5	16¼	15	12½	4,300	12	17½
Demi Culverin	4½	4¼	11¾	9	9	3,000	11	16⅜
Demi Cannon Lesse	4¼	4	9	8	7½	2,300	10	14⅜
Saker Ordinary	3¾	3½	5½	5½	5	1,900	9½	14
Sakeret or Minion	3¼	3	3¼	5	3½	1,100	8	11½
Fawcon	2¾	2½	2⅓	2½	2¼	750	7	10¼
Fawconet	2¼	2	1 1/7	1½	1½	400	6	8⅔
Rabinet	1½	1¼	¾	¾	2/4	300	5 2/4	7½
Base	1¼	1	⅓	⅓	¼	200	4 2/4	6½

*Too powerful for many pieces.

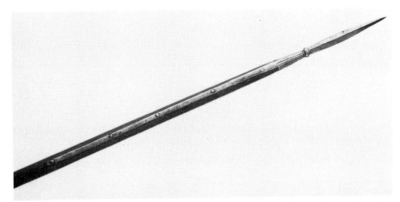

Head of a 17th Century pike. The blade has a lozenge section and is nearly a foot long including the socket. Note the long metal strips or 'languets' running for a couple of feet down the sides of the shaft to prevent the blade being chopped off (NAM).

cavalry ones). He probably wore very similar equipment to that of the infantry musketeer, apart from riding-boots, and was armed, preferably, with a flintlock musket (as were the New Model's dragoons); usually a light model, equipped with a sling and probably not requiring a rest.

Artillery

The accompanying table (from Ward) and illustrations show details of the artillery of the day. 'Cannon' were primarily short-range, wide-bore wall-breakers; mortars and perriers high-trajectory weapons, again for use against fortified places. The other guns, of 'culverin' type, were longer-barrelled and more suited to use as field pieces. Weapons of up to demi-cannon size were occasionally used in battle; demi-culverins and sakers were 'standard' field guns, while the smaller pieces were used in direct support of infantry units. The smaller guns were usually bronze, the cannon of iron, less dependable but infinitely cheaper. Battery guns — a kind of early attempt at a machine-gun, with several small barrels on the same carriage — were also sometimes used (the 88 'frames' carried by Leven's army were probably of this type), and the Royalists utilised a few 'galloper' guns, with fully mounted crew.

Guns mainly fired solid iron shot, but mortars threw explosive shells or 'granadoes'. 'Hail shot' was also used,

Thickness of the plank (ins)	Number of men to pull	Number of horses	Yoke of oxen	Range in paces Point blank	Range in paces Utmost random
8	90	16	9	300	1,500
7½	80	14	8	340	1,600
7¼	70	12	7	360	1,740
6¾	65	11	6	370	1,800
6½	60	10	5	350	1,700
6	56	9	5	340	1,600
5½	50	8	4	420	2,100
5¼	46	8	4	400	2,000
4½	36	7	4	380	1,800
4¼	28	6	3	320	1,600
3¾	24	5	3	300	1,500
3½	20	4	2	280	1,400
2¾	16	3	2	260	1,200
2¼	10	2	2	220	1,000
2	8	2	2	150	700
2	6	2	2	100	560

17th Century Scots claymore. Though somewhat reduced from the huge 16th Century type, it could still be wielded two-handed (DOE).

Field guns and carriage, from Henry Hexham, Principles of the Art Military *1639* (NAM).

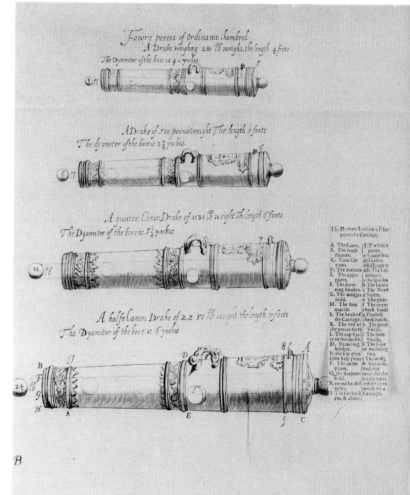

The English Civil War

particularly by the smaller infantry support pieces (this could be loose musket-balls or a more elaborate forerunner of case shot, with iron 'hail' in a lead container).

Performance of artillery was limited by inefficient powder (the 'corned' type used in small arms was too powerful for guns), inaccuracy ('windage' of ¼-inch between ball and bore was standard, and the dispart sight and gunners' quadrant employed in sieges could not be used in the field) and by low rates of fire. Canvas or paper cartridges were sometimes used, but the larger guns were always loaded with loose powder by ladle, from a 'budge-barrel' near the gun—a slow and dangerous process. According to William Eldred (*The Gunners Glasse*, 1646) 'One may well make 10 shots an hour if the peeces be well fortified and strong, but if they be ordinary peeces, then 8 is enough, always provided that after 40 shots you refresh and cool the peece, and let her reste an houre.' It seems that on average one gunner and one or two matrosses (assistants) were allotted to each gun, but for the larger ones they must have required the unskilled assistance of a considerable number of pioneers or infantrymen, and a train of artillery required hundreds of horses, wagons, carters, pioneers and craftsmen, the whole, as Clarendon remarked, being very expensive— 'Commonly a Spunge, that never can be filled or satisfied' and, on the unsurfaced roads of the day, very immobile (it should be remembered, however, that the train would normally include ammunition and ordnance services for the horse and foot as well).

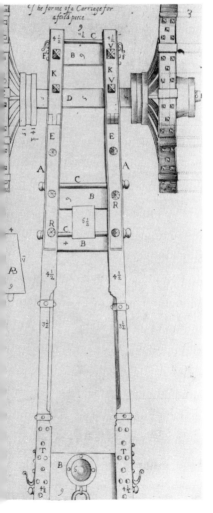

Siege weapons

We have no space here to go into detail on siege warfare—a subject in its own right—but some of the special devices used are worth a mention:

The Petard Used to blow down doors and gates, it consisted of a roughly conical metal container full of powder, having either a rim through which it could be screwed to the target, or a sort of wooden carriage which held it against the door while the fuse burnt down to the powder.

The Grenade Hollow iron sphere about three inches across and weighing up to 2½ lbs, filled with powder and ignited by fuse, just like the 'bomb' of the cartoonist. Used a lot in sieges, but not yet, apparently, in the field.

The Penthouse A musket-proof timber shelter on cartwheels, loopholed for shooting, allowing assault parties to advance under cover and capable of being used to bridge a ditch.

17th Century pikeman's sword (NAM).

The Fire-Pike Tie to a pike a canvas bag filled with gunpowder, linseed and turpentine, daub with pitch and allow to harden, then drill two holes near the top and fill with fine powder, to cause two jets of flame when ignited. Garnish to taste with loaded pistol-barrels, and, remarks Ward ghoulishly: 'This instrument will perform excellent service in a throng of people'. Certainly one seems to have had great moral effect at the Royalist taking of Bristol.

Four types of cannon with dimensions, showing gunners' tools (Hexham) (NAM).

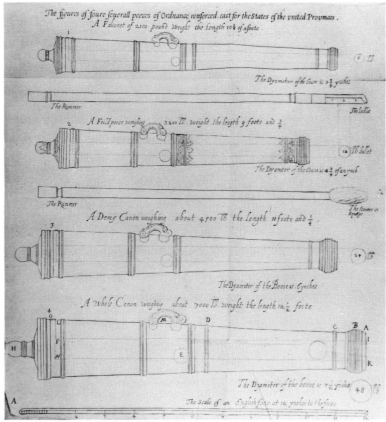

The English Civil War

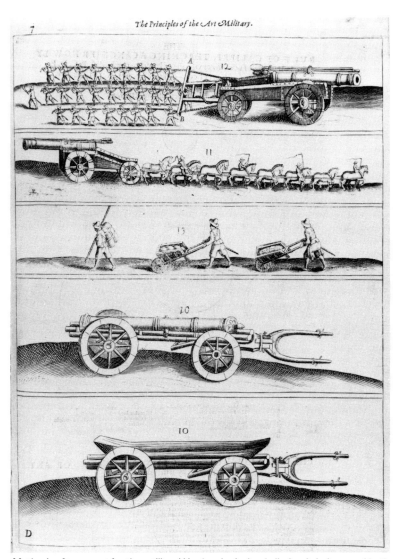

Methods of transport for the artillery (Hexham). A simple limber is being used in the second sketch from the top, with the then characteristic arrangement of one horse (usually the strongest) in shafts, and then pairs in the traces. The next picture down shows a heavy gun dismounted for carriage on a special wagon, and below it is a pontoon wagon (NAM).

Weapons and equipment   31

four

Organisation and tactics

The Foot

The 12 infantry regiments of the New Model Army were intended to be of 1,200 men in ten companies, 100-strong, except for those of the Colonel (200), Lieutenant-Colonel (160), and Major (140). The others were led by Captains. This was probably the general pattern aimed at in the Civil War, though in practice most regiments had fewer men—about 400 might be a typical strength—and some had fewer companies. On the battlefield, in any case, infantry were normally deployed in 'battaglia', ideally 500 to 600 strong; a regiment might, if strong, form two of these; if weak, only one or part of one. Each body of infantry would consist of both pikemen and musketeers. In the New Model there were two musketeers to each pikeman; the Covenanters used the Swedish ratio of 3:2, certain Royalist forces 4:3, while some of the London Trained Band regiments in 1643 had practically equal numbers of pikes and muskets.

Whatever their numbers, the pikes would be drawn up as the central body of each division or battalion, with the standards of the companies (and any halberdiers) placed in the centre of their ranks. The musketeers could draw up in front, as 'sleeves' on either flank, or all round the pikes. Elaborate Swedish formations appear in many contemporary books, but the simpler Dutch ones would seem better suited to the amateurish troops of the Civil War. However, the Dutch practice of drawing up the foot ten-deep was certainly replaced by the Swedish six ranks during the war.

The foot would march 'in order', with three feet between files, and often six feet between ranks, and the 'shot' might fight at the same spacing, but for receiving cavalry the pikes were recommended to pack together both by ranks and files, as closely as possible, almost like a rugby scrum, the first four ranks 'charging' their pikes braced on the ground (illustration, No 33—against infantry No 14 would be used). The rear ranks would have their pikes ported (No 13) or advanced (No 15), as they waited to fill gaps or join in a general mêlée. The deep formations not only allowed the serried points of four ranks of pikes to be presented at the enemy, but also allowed the shot to keep up a steady fire, by giving them time to reload.

This could be achieved by the individual files counter-marching: each man turning and going to the rear of his file after firing, so the whole formation moved slowly back—fire by 'extraduction', or each man walking up to the head of his file when ready to fire, so the unit moved forward—'introduction'. Ward says, however, that this method 'is not used (in these our Moderne Warres) but in way of exercise,' and in the Civil War the standard method would seem to have been to give fire by ranks (or sometimes files), often led some way forward (or to the side or rear) from the body of their unit. After firing the whole rank would move to a flank, then wheel round behind their division to reload. Sometimes six foot gaps were left every five or six files to allow for this. This not only allowed continuous fire, but made it possible, for example, to maintain a screen of musketeers in front of the pikes, and fire could be directed to flank or rear with ease (in fact, contemporary military writers tended to be carried away by the possibilities into endless variations sounding more like country dances than military movements!) For increased fire effect, well trained musketeers could fire by 'Salve, powring on showers of lead, firing two or three ranks together'—in fact Elton (*The Compleat Body of the Art Military*,

Musket drill (Hexham) (NAM).

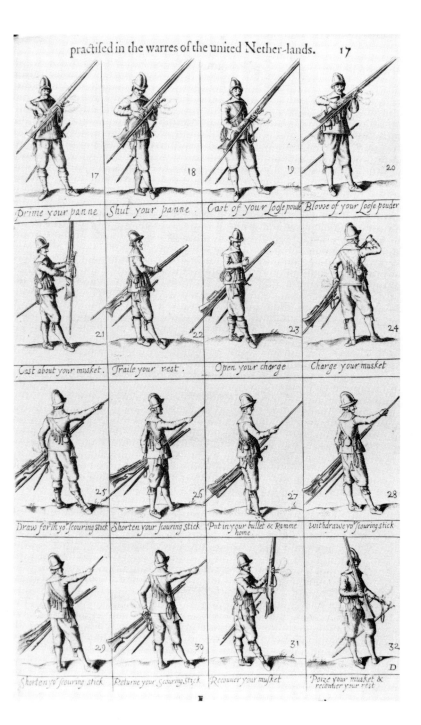

17	18	19	20
Prime your panne	*Shut your panne.*	*Cast of your loofe poude*	*Blowe of your loofe pouder*
21	22	23	24
Cast about your musket.	*Traile your rest.*	*Open your charge*	*Charge your musket*
25	26	27	28
Draw forth yo.r scouring stick	*Shorten your scouring stick*	*Put in your bullet & Ramme home.*	*Withdrawe yo.r scouring stick*
29	30	31	32
Shorten yo.r scouring stick	*Returne your scouring stick*	*Recouuer your musket*	*Poize your musket & recouuer your rest*

1650) suggests that up to *six* ranks could fire at once, but surely three would have been the practical limit—it seems to have been usual to draw out into three ranks for volley fire. Salvo was used by the New Model, by Hopton's men at Cheriton, and Montrose's troops (as a single volley before charging).

If threatened by horse, musketeers could kneel or crouch in front of the pikes, whose levelled points could protect a couple of ranks, but this would not, of course, protect *all* of them, so most would have to take refuge behind the pikemen, who sometimes left intervals for the purpose. On occasion pikes and muskets could actually be interspersed, as the Earl of Eglinton's

English musket exercises, 1600 (NAM).

The English Civil War

Regiment did at Marston Moor, or a 'Ring' rather like the later square could be formed, with a rank of pikes backing up two of musketeers.

In an advance, firing musketeers would usually be led somewhat in advance of the pikes and might, as noted, actually screen them, but when it came to 'push of pike' they would normally fall back to about mid-file where they could fire 'secure from the enemies pikes offending them'.

The Horse

Cavalry formed a much higher proportion of armies at this time than would be the case later, most writers recommending that they should form from a quarter to a third of the whole army. As can be seen from the historical summary, the proportion could even be higher.

The 11 cavalry regiments of the New Model were each composed of six 100-man troops, but earlier Parliamentary and Scots troops were supposed to be 60, then 80 strong. Six troops seems to have been standard for English armies, eight for the Covenanters, but commanders' own units were often larger. Prince Rupert's regiment, for instance, had ten troops and Cromwell's 14, for a strength of about 1,100. Royalist troops and regiments in particular tended to become understrength and, by 1645 the majority of regiments in the King's army were 100- or 150-strong, and the largest not over 400.

When the war started, some Parliamentary horse at least seem to have formed in Dutch order, five or six ranks deep — a formation primarily suited to giving fire by ranks, like the infantry. But as early as Edgehill Rupert was deploying the King's horse in the newer Swedish fashion of three ranks, and by the end of the war this was practically universal. This was unsuited to shooting, but ideal for shock action, bringing, as Bariffe observes, 'more hands to the fight'. The best men were placed in the front rank, to lead the charge, and the second best in the rear rank, to stop the worst — in the middle — running away! In the early days of the war there were cases of horse on both sides receiving charges at the halt, depending on their firearms, but this may have been simply inexperience. Rupert taught the Cavaliers to charge at the gallop with the sword, the pistols being fired at the last minute or reserved for the mêlée (according to Ward, the first shot should be at the opponent's belly, the second at his horse, and you should then go for his reins or the straps of his armour with your sword). The charge would start at the trot, and you were supposed to wait until 100 paces from the enemy 'and then fall into your careire', and it may be that some Parliamentary horse actually *delivered* the attack at the trot, which would make it easier to keep control.

The horse seem normally to have maintained a fairly open formation — Bariffe suggests four feet (enough for another horse) between files, and eight between ranks, but might charge knee-to-knee, while Haselrig's Lobsters evidently employed the close-packed order traditional for cuirassiers, at least at Roundway Down and, although routed there, they were very successful elsewhere. Cuirassiers were normally to attack at the trot, relying on their pistols rather than their swords.

On the field, regiments of horse were drawn up in a number of divisions or companies — what we would call squadrons — of varying sizes; they could be one, two or three troops strong, anything from 50 to 300 men. Usually those of one regiment would be drawn up in line, but sometimes in column, as some of Cromwell's seem to have been at Marston Moor.

Contemporary writings laid considerable stress on flexibility — no body of horse, whether a regiment or an isolated troop, should attack in one mass but, since 'the best and safest place to charge the enemie upon, is the flanks and reare', should if possible detach a force to attack the enemy flank while the main body engaged them frontally. Above all, a reserve should be kept: even a troop of but 50, if fighting

Overleaf *Pike drill* (*Hexham*) (NAM).

practised in the warres of the united Nether-lands.

1. Order yo.r Pike.
2. Aduance yo.r Pike in three motions. The first Motion.
3. the seacond Motion.
4. the third Motion being Aduanced.
5. Order yo.r Pike in 3 motions. the first Motion.
6. the 2.d Motion.
7. The 3.d motion being ordered.
8. Shoulder yo.r Pike in 3 motions. The first Motion.
9. The seacond Motion.
10. The 3.d motion being Sholdred.
11. Port yo.r Pike in 3 motions. the first motion.
12. The 2.d Motion.
13. The 3.d motion being Ported.
14. Charge yo.r Pike.
15. Aduance yo.r Pike.
16. Sholder yo.r Pike in 3 motions. The first Motion.

17

18

19

2o

The 2ᵈ motion.

The 3ᵈ motion being Sholdred

Charge to yᵉ Rearein 2 motions the first motion.

The 2ᵈ motion

21

22

23

24

The 3ᵈ motion being Charged.

Recouer yᵉ Pike and Shalder in 3 motions The first motion.

The feacond motion.

The 3ᵈ motion being Sholdred.

25

26

27

28

Order yᵒʳ Pike.

Cheeke yᵒ Pike the first motion.

The 2ᵈ motion being Cheeked.

Trayle yᵒ Pike.

29

30

31

32

33

Charg for horfe and draw yᵉ fword.

Recouer yᵒ Pike and Charge the firft Palming motion

The 2ᵈ Palming motion.

Charge yᵒ Pike.

Order at clofe Order.

Putap your fword & order yoᵘ Pike.

B

Pistol drill for the cuirassier, 1630 (Military Instructions for the Cavallrie) (NAM).

alone, should keep ten or 12 men back, since 'if they never so little disorder themselves, they cannot reassemble unless they have fresh men to sustain the enemy'. If charged by a stronger enemy, and with 'neither time nor convenience to put themselves in good order', they should scatter to evade the charge. Wargamers using reasonably advanced rules will recognise the soundness of this advice, but the same can't be said for another recommendation — that a formation might split in two and shoot up a charging enemy as he galloped obligingly through the gap between them!

Commands for all these manoeuvres were conveyed both by trumpet calls and by signalling with the standards.

Deploying an army

'The Ordering or Embattelling of an Army for to fight, is the Chiefest of all Military Actions' (Bariffe).

For at least the set-piece battle in reasonably open terrain, there was a well-established pattern for drawing up an army.

The main body of infantry forming the centre would be disposed, as mentioned, in 'battaglia', usually in three lines — a vanguard, 'main battell' and 'line of succour' (support line), according to Ward. The lines were separated by at least 20 paces, and the battalions from their neighbours by at least ten. They were often disposed chequer-fashion, with the battalions in the rear rows covering the gaps between those in front, and in such case the gaps were sometimes made wide enough for the battalions to advance or fall back through them. There might be a small final reserve of both horse and foot behind the last line. For command purposes the foot were often divided into three 'brigades' or 'tertias', but these, like the battalions, were *ad hoc* battlefield arrangements rather than permanent ones.

The horse would be placed, roughly equally, upon either flank of the foot for, as Ward observes, 'Unlesse your

The English Civil War

strength in horse doe much exceed the Enemies, it will be to your disadvantage to strive to charge the Enemies foot troops (unlesse there should be an unexpected advantage offered) until such time as you have either routed the Enemies horse, or put them to flight, and then you are to assault them upon all quarters' — an accurate prediction of what happened in most of the Civil War battles. The prime task of the cavalry was to see off their opposite numbers, and thus they were usually found in the centre only as a final reserve. Ward warns that 'In the meane time they must have a sleeve of horse upon each flank of the wings of the foot troops, to defend them from the Enemies charge, who will adventure to do it, when they see them left naked.' He suggests a gap of at least 100 paces between the horse and the flank of the infantry, and a minimum spacing of 25 paces between companies (squadrons) and 50 between regiments.

Like the foot, the horse were ideally formed into three lines or 'battles'. Bariffe suggests concentrating their strength forward, with the following proportionate strengths: first line, ten; second, five; third, three; and general reserve, four. Squadrons were often arranged chequer-fashion, and those of the 'line of succour' were more widely spaced, to allow those ahead to retire through them if necessary.

A Swedish practice quite often used, was to place small bodies of 'commanded' musketeers (ie, men detailed for duty separately from their regiments) in the intervals of the cavalry squadrons, particularly in the first line, their duty being to disorder the enemy with their fire, then fall back into the intervals of the second line.

The heaviest cavalry — cuirassiers, if there were any — were supposed to be placed closest to the infantry, or in the rear line.

The commander of the wing most often seems to have taken personal command of the first line, with his second-in-command leading the next, and groups of squadrons might be temporarily brigaded together for command purposes on the field. In fact, by 1645 the King's army appears to have developed a semi-permanent brigade

Company in the Dutch order, from Hexham. The musketeers are firing by ranks, and then marching to the rear two ranks at a time (NAM).

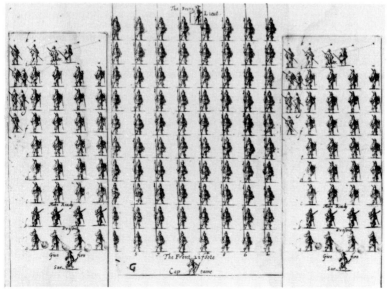

organisation, the brigades of horse being 750 to 850 strong—a remarkably advanced step for the day.

It must be remembered, of course, that the placing and movements of the horse would be particularly affected by terrain. Although England was much more open than today, there were many battles, like Cheriton for example, where hedged fields or lanes affected cavalry movements with drastic results. Although hunting gentry might clear hedges, ordinary troopers were not usually trained to jump, and their horses were heavily loaded. At Nantwich, Fairfax had pioneers who gapped the hedges for his cavalry, but this does not seem to have been common. Ward, in fact, suggests that if one wing is well-provided with natural obstacles, no cavalry should be stationed there at all.

Dragoons, on the other hand, revelled in natural obstacles, 'They being chiefly to secure Passes and to line Hedges, if occasion requires, either to secure the other cavalry with whom they march, or to offend the Enemy'. Most armies would have a smallish number present, either in their own regiments, similar to those of foot, or sometimes in single troops attached to cavalry regiments. Their main service was really *off* the battlefield, acting as advanced and rear guards, escorts and outposts, but they could also do a useful job *on* it. They were nearly always on the extreme flanks, occupying hedges or copses, from which they could harass an advancing enemy with their fire, but could also be called on to give mobile fire support to cavalry attacking infantry, and might even on rare occasions charge a disordered enemy themselves, as Okey's men did at Naseby.

It was usual to place a 'forlorn hope' to cover the front of the army: a thin line of 'commanded' musketeers well in advance, taking advantage of any available hedges, ditches, etc, and aiming to irritate and delay an advancing enemy; if not under cover, they might advance individually to fire, falling back again to load, or could even march slowly in a large circle, firing when reaching the point nearest to the enemy. According to Bariffe, when forced to retire (as they certainly would be), the forlorn should fall back into the intervals of the main body and hold themselves in readiness to attack the flanks of enemy battalions.

Finally, and in some ways the most difficult question: where to put the artillery? If there happened to be high ground in rear, the guns could be placed there—usually widely spaced out rather than concentrated in batteries (they had no unit organisation below that of the train itself). If not, they could be put in front of the foot, with a good view of the enemy, but in a vulnerable position (a recommended tactic was to have a body of loosely formed horse and foot ready to rush enemy guns early on, so if they *were* exposed they were supposed to be provided with an infantry guard. Gunners were armed with linstocks or halberds, matrosses with half-pikes, but their powers of self-defence would be limited). Alternatively they could be between brigades, or on the flanks of the foot.

For the lighter guns, Elton suggested they could be spaced at 50- to 100-foot intervals in front of the infantry battalions to discourage enemy charges, being readily withdrawn, with drag ropes, into the intervals of the infantry line when threatened. Occasionally they were even placed with the forlorn hope.

The English Civil War

five

Wargaming the Civil War

There is a lot to be said for this period as a setting for wargames. For a start, there are plenty of books available, both on the battles and the armies, and the would-be wargamer should find plenty to help him paint his miniature armies, although at the same time he will be able to follow his personal taste much more than with, say, Napoleonic forces, uniformity during the Civil War being somewhat limited (the wargamer would be well advised to make his regiments as uniform as historically possible — basically one coat colour for each — since this will greatly speed up painting). Accurate flags, too, will present no problem, and since each company and troop had its own, the armies can be more flag-bedecked and colourful than those of other periods. Ten to an infantry regiment would probably not be very practical, but several per unit not only look good, but are handy if you want to split the regiment into two or more bodies, a thoroughly historical procedure which gives useful flexibility to your Civil War armies, if you make the regiments reasonably large. A similar advantage, incidentally, is that practically any unit (save perhaps Lord Brook's Purplecoats and Haselring's Cuirassiers) *could* be used for either side, provided you don't stick to the identifying sash colours, red and orange (which were in reality *not* universal), in which case you should also provide yourself with some spare cavalry cornets, since one really can't have Parliamentarians going into battle under flags making insulting reference to the Earl of Essex's marital problems, or Cavaliers bearing anti-episcopal slogans!

An army of this period is not only very colourful, but looks, when deployed on the table, extraordinarily like contemporary battle-prints, with their formally-disposed blocks of pike and squadrons of horse. The generally small armies, small battlefields, short ranges and rather stereotyped dispositions and tactics of the day are very well suited to the wargame, while the interdependence of musket and pike sets interesting tactical problems, and the numbers and striking power of the horse make for lively and decisive games.

At present, the only ready-made model soldiers available are lead ones, but there are plenty of these, and the excellent 15 mm ranges put out by Peter Laing and Miniature Figurines give a comprehensive selection of cheap figures. The more expensive, but individually more attractive, 25 mm figures are available from Hinton Hunt, Warrior, Miniature Figurines, Garrison and Hinchliffe (as manufacturers' millimetres seem to differ a good bit, I have listed these in rising order of average size, but most figures of the latter four at least can be combined within your army). There may be some Phoenix (20 mm) and Tradition figures still around too, and in the USA Grenadier Figures turn out a sizeable range.

Unfortunately, Airfix do not yet produce any OO/HO Cavaliers and Roundheads, but it is quite possible to build up plastic Civil War armies from the figures they *do* make, favourites for the horse being the French cuirassiers, while for the foot any with breeches, and puttees or boots which can simply be painted as Civil War stockings, can be used (the World War 1 Americans usefully combine these with a broad-brimmed hat).

Space here does not permit going into the converting, or, for that matter, painting of wargames figures; the techniques, however, will be much the same for any period, and guidance, if needed, can be found in *Modelling Miniature Figures*, edited by Bruce Quarrie (Patrick Stephens Ltd).

Whatever troops you decide to use, a further advantage of Civil wargaming is that you can manage with a smallish number of them. Not, that is, if you want to reconstruct the larger battles, but many Civil War armies and engagements were very small, and the large amount of localised warfare offers an excellent field for the use of quite modest forces. An army of a couple of regiments of foot which, if you use the popular one model to 20 real soldiers ratio, might be 20 to 30 figures; three or four squadrons of horse (which could easily be only five or six strong); a gun and, of course, a general (Warrior, Miniature Figurines and Hinchliffe all make personality figures, including the King, Prince Rupert, Cromwell and Fairfax) will give just as interesting a game as a larger force.

The most interesting wargames are usually those which result from a campaign fought on maps, where all kinds of vital matters may hang upon the result of the battle, and forces may be unbalanced so that a weaker side, say, may have to conduct a fighting retreat until reinforcements come up from an unexpected direction.

Again the Civil War lends itself well to this sort of thing. I would advocate a purely local affair, which could be based on one of the contemporary county maps obtainable remarkably cheaply, for example, from the British Museum;

preferably using one's own county. The map will give towns, villages, houses, and sometimes woods and hills; roads may need to be added, sparingly, from a more modern one. If you lean to research, much of the background could in many areas be historical; otherwise a dice-throw system can decide the loyalties of individuals (like landowners) or groups (such as town and village populations), giving some regard to probability, so that a manufacturing town, for example, is more likely to be Parliamentarian. Either way, you will get a confused and interesting situation for your campaign, especially if you start with most weapons located at certain militia armouries and great houses, and initial recruits with improvised weapons only. Making control of areas the key to income and recruitment, as is often done in campaigns, is entirely appropriate to such a Civil War situation. You can have a fine mix of troop types too, with well-trained 'regulars', local militia, great magnates and their retainers, and ill-armed peasantry (several manufacturers produce them!).

A couple of points on the map-moving and map-contacts side of such a campaign. *March speeds*—an average day's march for a substantial force of

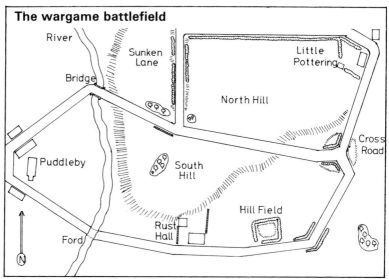

The wargame battlefield

River

Sunken Lane

Little Pottering

Bridge

North Hill

Puddleby

South Hill

Cross Road

Hill Field

Rust Hall

Ford

N

The English Civil War

The field on move 3, with Little Pottering in the foreground; the Royalists have not yet appeared, and the convoy and escort are moving up the north and centre roads. Beyond the crossroads, Colonel Dove's horse are deploying, while in the left middle distance Sir John Smythe's men can be discerned, climbing the slope from Rust Hall.

horse, foot, and guns would be ten miles, but 12 was common and Fairfax, on his way to relieve Taunton in 1645 with 10,000 men and artillery, in hot weather, did 113 miles in a week. *Scouting and discovering enemy forces* — very poor; 'Scoutmasters' tended to be quite junior officers and cavalry, although occasionally 'commanded' for the purpose, not often used for reconnaissance and not trained for it.

Finally, the 'software' for English Civil Wargaming is also readily available. Sets of rules on sale are listed in the appendix, and there is a Pike and Shot Society which caters for enthusiasts, wargaming or otherwise, for the whole period of 16th and 17th Century military history. It holds local meetings and an AGM, and provides a bi-monthly magazine, *The Arquebusier*, generally carrying a preponderance of English Civil War material, both historical and wargaming.

To show the possibilities, we now turn to take a brief look at an actual game, a smallish action of the type which might (but didn't) arise in a Civil War campaign. The honest and unbiased author chose to use the Wargames Research Group rules for the period (which he wrote) and, as umpire, set up a typical little action between two local players: Malcolm Dove who, in the character of Colonel Praise the Lord and Fear Not Dove, ex-draper of Norwich, was responsibile for the safe passage of a convoy containing powder and £10,000 pay from Little Pottering to Puddleby (see map); and Clive McLeod who, elevated for the purpose to a baronetcy, was dispatched by His Majesty's Council of War to intercept. The fiendish umpire provided each player with a general order giving his task, and limited information on enemy and friendly forces. The rules class troops into 'A' (brave but undisciplined aristocrats), 'B' (excellent troops like the Ironsides), 'C' (ordinary), 'D' (poorly trained or irregular) and 'E' (ugh!), but our players were told merely that a unit was 'reliable', 'in arrears of pay' and so on, only discovering its exact class when the moment arrived to take a Reaction Test (to see what a unit will do at moments of stress—first close approach to enemy, first under artillery fire, receiving heavy losses, seeing friends run and so on—and their behaviour depends on their class as well as the situation). Further uncertainties, settled by the umpire throwing dice, were whether the Royalists would be able to raise the loyal citizen of Little Pottering and whether the Parliamentary commander of their troops at Rust Hall, the notorious Sir John Smythe, would be sober enough to follow Colonel Dove's orders. The rules make players—like real generals of the day—write general orders for each unit at the outset of a game, which will govern its actions throughout (unless the player's personal figure joins it or sends it new orders) and, as in real life, this is normally done when the armies have deployed, in sight of each other, within 120 paces (12 inches in the ground scale used) of their own edges of the table. In our present case, however, the unfortunate commanders had to write orders *before* the Royalists appeared—the exact moment for which the umpire kept to himself!

The four moves before the appearance of the Royalist horse revealed Colonel Dove's plans: two wagons and a gun, with the train guard, taking the North Road, the rest the centre route, covered by the Green Regiment at the crossroad and the Colonel's horse and dragoons to the south; the Puddleby garrison also moved toward the centre, and even Sir John proved to be having one of his better days, sending his foot to South Hill and leading the new-raised men off to guard the ford (as 'E's, Colonel Dove wisely intended to get them as far from the foe as possible).

All too soon the Royalist horse appeared—luckily for their commander *not* dashing off to the attack prematurely on their initial reaction tests as 'A' types are only too prone to do. Sir Clive sent his dragoons down the South Road in an attempt to outflank the Roundheads, a plan which failed a couple of moves later, when fire from their Parliamentary counterparts, lurking in Hill Field, caused a Reaction Test; being a bit isolated, with few pluses for friendly units within 150 paces, they decided to retire in disorder—a reaction which lasts three moves and means they abandon their original orders, and effectively put them out of the game, their beloved commander being *far* too occupied to give

Move 5. The Royalist horse have just appeared, and one body charge the Green musketeers at the crossroads.

The English Civil War

them any more, in true Prince Rupert style.

On the other flank, the Royalists were far more successful. Sir Clive's weakest regiment of horse overran the rather inadequately protected wagons (drivers, who were just hired civilians, will not offer resistance) and, despite the fact that one proved to have £4,000 aboard, declined to fall to looting (a possible reaction when horse or ill-disciplined foot get near baggage trains and the like). The firelocks of the train guard — in the field beside the road — did considerable damage, causing no less than 20 casualties in a move (one actual figure, casualties being assessed according to the 20:1 ratio of men represented by a figure. Firelocks are more effective at closer range because of their rate of fire, but not at long range, where the lack of a rest might well cancel this out). The musketeers wisely declined to charge the horse when their commander attempted to make them do so, but were not in too much danger from the cavalry owing to the hedge (you can only get extra effects from a charge over open ground,

and horse crossing a hedge would be disorganised — giving their opponents a hefty plus two in a hand-to-hand fight). Having rallied (which takes one or more moves after a mêlée, charge or similar, according to the class of the troops), the Royalist horse cantered on, rather *too* bravely for, entering the sunken road, they received hailshot from the gun, which had taken a full move to deploy ready to fire (in these rules, guns fire every move, since they represent several real pieces, but the low rate of fire is allowed for by restricting their effects, this being easier to keep track of than intermittent firing would be). They also took flanking fire from the train-guard and long-range fire from Smythe's foot in the centre (muskets being allowed a maximum range of 300 paces — 250 yards) and, not surprisingly, broke and fled (minuses for losses, disorganisation from fire, enemies within 150 paces, and to flank and rear, under artillery fire, fired on by ten figures etc, and *no* friends within 150. It is vital to keep units well supported). They did eventually rally near Little Pottering, encouraged by the sight of the villagers

Move 8. In the foreground, Colonel Dove's two squadrons, supported by dragoons on their right, are attacked by some Royalist horse. At the crossroads, the Green Regiment is in difficulties, its wings of musketeers driven away by cavalry charges, but Sir John Smythe's Foot can be seen forming a backstop further up the hill, while the left middle distance Parliamentary horse from Puddleby arrive to support their comrades.

A move later, things are seen from the Parliamentary side. In the foreground, Colonel Potts' Red Regiment holds the crest of South Hill as the wagons pass by. In the distance, left, the Train Guard face the Cavaliers rallying after taking the two wagons on the North Road, which are seen going to the rear under escort. The wretched carters cower in the Sunken Lane.

During the next move (the wagons have not yet been moved, although other troops have) the Parliamentary dragoons, have disposed of their Royalist opposite numbers, skirmish forward from Hill Field. Beyond, the cavalry mêlée continues, one Parliamentary squadron (left centre) having been driven back, but rallying under the personal leadership of Colonel Dove, who can be seen at the further end of their line. The Green Regiment, temporarily free from cavalry attack, is beginning to fall back.

The English Civil War

marching out in the King's cause, but on this flank things then died down into a long-range exchange of fire, involving the Royalist galloper gun, Sir Clive being afraid to allow either the 'E' class villagers or the shaken cavalry far from the shelter of the village.

In the centre, however, the main struggle developed. Perhaps unwisely, two Royalist bodies of horse were allowed to become involved with the Green Regiment at the crossroads; they made the musketeers run but, as sub-units these troops could rally automatically in the shelter of their pikes (too tough a proposition for the cavalry, since pikemen, unlike other troops, count their second rank as well as the first in any mêlée, *and* get plusses for ranks behind that). The Greens took losses and began to retire, but this could have been achieved by the Royalist musketeers (arriving on move 8). The cavalry were badly cut up and, since one of these units, and another sent north of the crossroads, were not involved, Sir Clive found himself with equal rather than superior numbers for the main mounted clash which took place a little to the south; otherwise, his victory would have been almost certain, the last reserve settling most cavalry fights on the table, as well as historically.

Even as it was, the Cavaliers almost brought it off, benefitting from the plus one that 'A' troops get in their first charge, and the fact that some of Parliament's horse were close-order fellows, advancing at a spiritless trot and thus getting only plus one for charging against the dashing Royalist's plus two. The slope of the hill evened things up a bit, though, and it was only Sir Clive's personal involvement (General fighting in the front rank = plus two on chance factor) that turned the scale. Two Roundhead units were routed—a sight (minus two on reaction for each friend in rout) which caused the Green Regiment, charged by some other horse, to turn and run too.

With this (move 11) Colonel Dove's position became distinctly fraught. Although his dispositions were quite strong—the wagons disappearing over the crest of South Hill, Colonel Potts' Regiment on the crest, and beside them his one remaining body of horse, rallying; Smythe's foot halfway down the hill, astride the centre road, and the train guard and artillery holding the Sunken Road—he had two cavalry and

Move 11. The cavalry mêlée and the Parliamentarian line, Rust Hall in the foreground.

Move 12 or thereabouts. The Greens are now in full retreat, while next to them the triumphant Cavaliers crash into Captain Partridge's horse, having routed their late opponents, the remnants of whom can be seen in full flight to the left rear. In the right foreground, the Royalist commanded musketeers pepper the Parliamentary foot from the banks round the crossroads, while Sir Clive's Life Guard, reduced to two figures by enemy fire, retire from the field past a number of rather depressing Royalist dice throws!

A move later—the crisis! The Greens, now broken, pour in panic through the ranks of Smythe's Foot, while a large Royalist hand moves up fresh horse against the latter. To the left, the Cavaliers have broken Captain Partridge's men (seen fleeing over the crest in the distance) but Colonel Dove has personally led his last mounted unit into the disordered Royalists, a move which will save the day.

The English Civil War

Same move—the main Parliamentary position. In the background, the artillery and Train Guard defend the Sunken Lane, while in the centre foreground Captain Partridge's horse flee past the Red Regiment, holding firm on the crest despite the appearance of the panic-stricken Greens on their other flank. Despite the dangerous situation, the precious convoy is nearing the river and comparative safety.

one infantry unit in flight, the Royalists having lost only one, and he was coming under heavy fire from the Royalist musketeers; his 'D' class troops could hardly be feeling very confident. No battle—or wargame—is lost until it is over, though, and the Colonel was, wisely, *not* conceding victory just yet.

Three things saved him. Firstly, the terrain gave the Green Regiment a chance to rally—once over the crest they would be out of sight, and sheltered from fire. Rally they did, and although the rules stipulated that they had hurled away their pikes and half their muskets during their panic flight, making them not much of a fighting force, at least their presence would now encourage rather than discourage their friends.

Secondly, his own actions. A General may take personal command of a unit, overriding its orders, and Colonel Dove led his last cavalry downhill into Sir Clive's advancing, triumphant, but disordered horse. The two Generals cancelled each other out and, after a drawn fight, both sides fell back to rally (compulsory after two moves of cavalry

mêlée with no result, it being evisaged that such a fight would not usually go on for long).

Thirdly, there was the magnificent conduct (or high dice-throwing, if you want to be prosaic) of Sir John Smythe's Regiment. Exposed as they were, they maintained excellent morale, calmly opening their ranks to let the routing Greens through; their musketeers successfully dodging a cavalry charge on their left flank (musketeer sub-units can and indeed *should* attempt to evade if charged by horse) and consistently throwing a plus chance factor when firing. This may not have depressed the little lead Royalists, but it certainly irritated their flesh-and-blood commander, who placed his General figure at the head of a rallied cavalry unit and led it in a charge on the right flank of Smythe's gallant men. It looked nasty, few pikes, but a distressingly large number of vulnerable musketeers being involved. However, Colonel Dove also dashed to the spot, and with his leadership (and plus two on the chance dice!) Smythe's infantry hurled back the horse with heavy loss, in fact three

End of the game. In the foreground, the two captured wagons stand in Little Pottering High Street, while in the fields around the village the inhabitants, some musketeers, and the Galloper Gun engage the enemy. In the distance, a body of Royalist horse turns to run after the wounding of Sir Clive, while another, rallying after an evaded charge, hovers menacingly on the left flank of Sir John Smythe's Regiment. Beyond, on the crest of the hill in front of Puddleby, gleam the pike points of the Parliamentary Red and Green Regiments (the latter now rallying after their rout, so for wargames purposes, those pikes have been thrown away!)

casualties per figure, and thus also three on the *General's* figure (which represents the leader himself, plus 19 cronies, toadies, staff officers and Life Guards). The penalty of too much personal conflict now arose — Sir Clive would have to throw a dice to see if he himself was wounded. A score at least equal to the number of casualties on his figure this move would save him. He threw; both Generals craned over the table to see the score — a two! Sir Clive's figure would now have to quit the field, losing all personal control of his men, while all who saw the mournful sight would be affected to the tune of minus two on subsequent reactions. Sadly, he ordered the signal for general retreat (players are allowed four signals, written down with orders at the start of the game). With but one move (the 16th) before dark, the Parliamentarians were safe.

They had not achieved a total victory, though, for Sir Clive had inflicted heavy losses, and withdrawn with a wagon-load of powder and £4,000 in coin. The wounded hero should be sure of a welcome in Oxford!

Even this small action had many engagements and episodes which have had to be omitted from such a brief account, but I hope it has given at least some idea of the possibilities, and particular flavour, of wargames in this period. Certainly, its course was remarkably similar to that which a real action might have followed.

There follow the army-lists used in the battle, with some sample lists for reasonably typical forces of the period (classification of troops is that of the WRG rules, which include a points system for choosing different, yet equally matched, forces).

Note: each force would have a

The English Civil War

commander, costing an additional 100 points, and might be provided with a baggage train (which costs no points to its owner, but will lose him 75 if lost, 25 if looted).

EHC = extra-heavy cavalry—three-quarter armour.

HCC, HI = heavy cavalry—corselet; heavy infantry—in breast and back plates.

MC, MI = medium cavalry, medium infantry—buff coat, jack, mail shirt and similar.

LI = light infantry—no protection.

(All troops are assumed to have swords).

The wargame armies

Colonel Dove's Roundheads	Points
His own horse: 2 squadrons, each of 7 HCC, 'C', pistols, order	230
The Puddleby Garrison:	
Colonel Potts' Red Regiment of Foot: 10 MI, 'D', pike, close order and 16 LI, 'D', musket, order, in two sub-units	140
Captain Partridge's Horse: 8 HCC, 'D', pistols, close order	122
At Rust Hall, under Sir John Smythe:	
Sir John Smythe's Regiment of Foot: 10 HI, 'D', pike, close order and 20 LI, 'D', musket, order, in two sub-units	170
New-raised men: 20 LI, 'E', sword or improvised weapon only	30
Convoy escort:	
Green Regiment of Foot: 12 HI, 'C', pike, close order and 24 LI, 'C', musket, order, in two sub-units	236
Train guard: 10 LI, 'C', firelocks, order	80
Dragoons: 10 MI, 'D', musket, horse	90
Artillery: 1 light gun, 3 'C' crew	58
Total:	**1,156**

Sir Clive McLeod's Royalists	Points
His Life Guard of horse: 5 HCC, 'B', pistols, order	90
3 squadrons of horse each 10 HCC, 'A', pistols, order	510
1 squadron of 10 MC, 'C', pistols, order	120
Dragoons: 8 MI, 'C', musket, with horses	82
Commanded musketeers: 3 units, each of 10 LI, 'C', musket, in order	210
Galloper gun: 1 light gun, 3 'C' crew, with horses	64
Countryfolk of Little Pottering: 10 LI, 'E', pole weapons; sub-unit of 5 LI, 'E', muskets; all in order	55
Total	**1,131**

Sample lists

Early Parliamentarian army	Points
2 regiments, each of 10 HCC, 'D', pistols, close order	300
1 regiment of 10 MC, 'D', pistols, close order	110
1 unit of cuirassiers: 6 EHC, 'C', pistol, close order	112
1 unit of dragoons: 6 MI, 'C', firelocks, horses	70
Artillery: 2 medium guns, 8 'C' crew	123
5 regiments, each of 10 HI, 'C', pike, close order and 16 LI, 'C', musket, order, in two sub-units	780
Total:	**1,495**

Royalist army

	Points
2 regiments, each of 10 HCC, 'A', pistols, order, each including one sub-unit	350
2 regiments, each of 10 MC, 'A', pistols, order, with sub-units	270
3 units, each of 5 MC, 'A', sword only, order	165
1 unit of dragoons: 5 MI, 'C', firelocks, horses	60
Artillery: 1 medium gun, 4 'C' crew	74
1 regiment of 10 HI, 'B', pike, close order, and 12 LI, 'B', musket, order, in two sub-units	174
1 regiment of 10 MI, 'C', pike, close order, and 12 LI, 'C', musket, order, in two sub-units	142
1 regiment of 8 MI, 'C', pike, close order, and a sub-unit of 8 LI, 'C', musket, order	103
1 regiment of 8 MI, 'D', pike, close order, and 12 LI, 'D', musket, order in two sub-units	112
Unit of new recruits: 20 LI, 'E', order, pole arms	50
Total:	**1,500**

Scots Covenanters

	Points
2 regiments, each of 10 MC, 'C', pistols, order, one sub-unit	250
2 squadrons of lancers, each of 5 MC, 'C', lance, pistol, order	160
Fraser's Dragoons: 6 MI, 'B', firelock, horse, capable of fighting mounted	82
Artillery:	
2 heavy guns, 12 'C' crew	167
2 battery guns, 6 'C' crew (each is a sub-unit of a foot regiment)	96
1 regiment of 8 HI, 'C', pike, close order, and 12 LI, 'C', musket, order, in two sub-units	140
1 regiment of 8 MI, 'C', pike, close order, and 12 LI, 'C', musket, order in two sub-units	132
3 regiments, each of: 8 MI, 'D', pike, close order, and 12 LI, 'D', musket, order, in two sub-units	336
2 units of Highlanders:	
12 MI, 'D', two-handed axe, order	58
14 LI, 'D', longbow, sword and buckler, order	80
Total:	**1,501**

Montrose

	Points
Gordon Horse: 6 MC, 'A', pistols, order	82
3 regiments of Irish, each of: 25 LI, 'B', fanatic, musket (can fire salvos), two-handed sword or axe, order with 2 sub-units	810
Highlanders:	
20 LI, 'D', longbow, sword and buckler, order	110
15 LI, 'D', longbow, sword and buckler, order	85
24 MI, 'A', musket, sword and buckler, order	250
12 MI, 'A', two-handed axe, order	82
12 MI, 'A', two-handed axe, order	82
Total:	**1,501**

Later Parliamentary army

	Points
5 squadrons, each of: 7 HCC, 'B', pistols, order	610
Dragoons: 5 MI, 'B', firelock, horse, capable of fighting mounted	70
2 regiments, each of: 8 HI, 'B', pike, close order, and 16 LI, 'B', musket (able to fire salvos), order, in two sub-units	408
2 regiments, each of: 6 HI, 'B', pike, close order, and 12 LI, 'B', musket (able to fire salvos), order, in two sub-units	316
2 light guns, 5 'C' crew	95
Total:	**1,499**

The English Civil War

six

Modelling Civil War figures

Before describing specific models made up from the Airfix 54 mm Collectors' Series kits now available—musketeer, pikeman and cavalryman—a few general observations on the dress of this period may be useful. The watchword for modellers in this period is variety; you can never be wrong by modifying details slightly from figure to figure, and those who are handy with putty, plastic card, plastic 'soup' and the faithful knife can have a lot of fun producing very individual figures.

First, the general cut of mid-17th Century clothes. Shirts of white or off-white material, varying in quality from coarse linen to fine silk and lace depending on social rank and wealth, were cut with generously baggy sleeves gathered at the wrist, and with broad turn-down collars. Often laced or scalloped cuffs were turned back up the wrist over the sleeves of the doublet. This was usually collarless, waist-length, and fastened up the front with many buttons. Again, sleeves were generous in cut. The fashion-conscious sometimes had the doublet sleeves slashed vertically into strips, to show the shirt beneath. Breeches were baggy and knee-length; often the fashionable had them fastened up the outside of each leg with many buttons. Knee-stockings were worn, and over-stockings or 'boot hose' were often worn over these, with the tops turned down. Laced shoes with a square toe, a rather high heel and a high front tongue were common, the quality and orna-mentation depending on wealth. Riders wore huge 'bucket-top' boots.

The military costumes of the day reflected this general appearance. Doublets and breeches in the colours of the regiment are frequently mentioned, although not in enough detail for us to be very confident when it comes to painting models. We know that the Earl of Manchester's Parliamentary regiment wore green coats lined red—but exactly how the red lining showed, we don't know. The same goes for Lord Monta-gue's regiment—how do we interpret 'red coats faced white'? What facings? We may assume that some units had coats and breeches of matching colours but, given the conditions of outfitting, and campaigning, it may well have been a rarity to see men of one regiment all with matching doublets and breeches.

Headgear varied widely, and the Hollywood image of the long-haired cavalier in a plumed slouch hat facing a grimly-cropped Puritan in a 'lobster-tail pot' is rubbish. The slouch hat, of all colours, qualities, and degrees of ornamentation, was simply the normal headgear of the 17th Century man who expected to be out in the weather. Both sides wore them, officers and men, foot and horse alike. Likewise, the 'pot' helmet was worn in battle by both Royalist and Roundhead; and not only by cavalry, either. Contemporary illustrations show infantry officers

Civil War infantry standard—third captain's company (NAM).

wearing them. The detailed variations of these basically similar helmets were also enormous. Some had smooth crowns, some were vertically fluted; some had three bar face-cages, some a single central bar, and some no bars at all. Some had vestigial spikes on top of the crown; some had deep laminated side-flaps, some small plain flaps; the length and shape of the peak and 'tail' varied widely. While a cavalry trooper's 'pot' might be plain dull steel, a wealthy officer might wear one with plumes, gilding, blueing—anything he could afford.

A similar range of difference could be seen in the popular 'buff coat'. Originally made from buffalo leather,

1641 infantry standard (blue and white apart from St George's cross. Possibly that of second captain's company) (NAM).

One type of buff coat; an early example dating from about 1620-30, it is unusual—as far as we know—in having a low standing collar. The body and skirts are of heavy ox-hide, while the sleeves are of much thinner leather, ringed with decorative strips of metallic braid—a common practice if contemporary illustrations are to be believed. The collar and cuffs are buttoned, while the body is closed by a series of metal clasps.

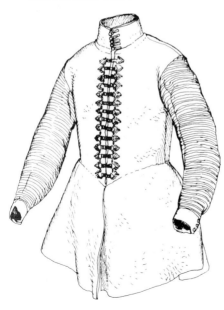

and by the Civil War generally of ox-hide, this heavy leather coat offered a comfortable padding between doublet and armour, and good protection against sword-cuts. Some were sleeveless, some had wrist-length sleeves of thinner leather or cloth. Some had a thin long sleeve, covered down to the elbow by a broad-cut over-sleeve of the heavier leather, slit or loosely laced at the bottom to allow elbow movement. Some had forearm-length over-sleeves with a plain or fancy cut-out on the inside of the elbow, for the same reason.

The buff coat is associated with cavalrymen, but was often worn by the foot as well. It offered a pikeman the same advantages as a trooper; and although unusual, it is not unknown to find illustrations of musketeers wearing them over their doublets. Where there was a full-length thin leather or cloth sleeve, it was often slit down the front seam and fastened with many buttons. When not required for warmth or protection the sleeves could be unbuttoned and allowed to hang down behind the shoulder. These long sleeves, of both buff coat and doublet, were often decorated with many transverse and some vertical bands of lace, ribbon or metallic braid. It is a misinterpretation of this effect in contemporary illustrations which has led to the popular image of Cromwell's troopers wearing Rugby shirts beneath

The English Civil War

their buff coats! In fact it is far safer to paint a Cromwellian trooper's sleeves plain red; we know the bulk of the New Model wore this colour from its formation onward.

When modelling such small items as hat-bands, plumes, knee-garters, gloves, stockings, shoes, belting, and so on, you may range from one end of the paint tray to the other without fear of authoritative criticism — for we simply don't know the answers. When in doubt, especially in the case of common soldiers, stick to the plainer, duller shades. Vegetable dyes were not particularly stable, so vary the colours subtly from man to man. Red, an expensive colour to produce, probably varied from bright scarlet to orange-brown. Use muted blues and greens, off-whites, various shades in the brown-to-grey range, pale yellows, and so forth. (Incidentally, don't mix greys from black and white alone — a touch of blue or brown achieves a softer effect.)

Buff coats can be in any of several shades, from reddish tan to beige to buff to yellow. Armour was very often painted black to protect it from rust, but unpainted dull steel would also be acceptable. When modelling officers and well-turned-out soldiers, remember the love of ornament of that period. Lace officers' sleeves in gold and silver, and add rows of tiny buttons; lace and button breeches as well. Gloves often had fringed cuffs, and belts would have the loose ends scalloped or cut into fancy shapes. Buckles and keeps would be of every metal and every shape. Don't overlook sword scabbards and hilts in your decorative frenzy! Boots sometimes — among the dandies — had red heels and red edges to the soles, and big butterfly spur-leathers. About the one coloured item we can be sure of is the sash frequently worn to distinguish friend from foe: orange-tawny for Parliament, rose-red for the King. Officers would quite often have fine bullion fringes on their sashes in gold or silver.

The length of hair — that tell-tale distinction beloved of Victorian and Hollywood legend — was, obviously, pretty random. Certainly, Puritan troops would probably keep their hair cut fairly plain and short — but Puritans were a minority in the New Model. The normal style of the day, for both sides, was similar to that seen in every British street today — a length somewhere between the nape and the collar-bone, and no significance can be attached to either extreme. Only a wealthy dandy, with a suite of servants following him on campaign, would bother with very long or elaborate hair in the middle of a war! The short beard and full moustache was the normal style of a gentleman, but clean-shaven men were no rarity on either side, we may be sure.

A final thought; to individualise your models, remember that temporary 'field signs' were a feature of the Civil War.

A simpler, classic pattern of buff coat of 1630-40; remember that much material of rather advanced age was pressed into service during the Civil War. Armour and weapons of the latest pattern did not exist in any large standing stocks; armouries and magazines all over the country were stripped, and as the war progressed much was imported from the Continent, so many national styles may be seen in the way of helmet design, pistol shape and furniture, and so on. This coat has the body and overlapping skirts, and the half-length oversleeves, in heavy leather laced together at breast and elbow, and thin, flexible, full-length undersleeves.

These were sprigs of greenery in the helmet, coloured cloths tied round the arm, sashes—even shirt-tails hanging out the back!

And so, to the kits:

The musketeer

This attractive figure can be made up straight from the kit instructions, with three reservations. Follow the sequence shown in the instructions. Start by joining the two halves of the torso, filling with 'soup'* and filing along any visible join-line. Join and finish the two legs in the same way; then join torso and leg assemblies. After dealing with the slung equipment (see below) add the collar to the torso, the head to the collar

*'Soup': for a description of this useful material, see Airfix Magazine Guide 19: *Model Soldiers*.

and the hat to the head. If you plan a number of slightly differing figures together in a diorama, you can ring the changes slightly on the heads by substituting the slouch-hatted head from the mounted figure kit, and/or making a hat or two from scratch using the cut-down crown from a 95th Rifles kit shako, and a plastic card brim softened and bent to shape. Choose arms to suit the preferred pose, and 'offer' these, the musket, and the rest up to the main assembly and base— perhaps sticking temporarily with Plasticine—until you find a convincing angle, before sticking the parts permanently in place. The kit provides arms with gauntlets—we feel this is rather unconvincing for a musketeer, and suggest you file off the cuffs and cut a wrist into the plastic to give the effect of

Musketeer, modified slightly with arms from the spares box, and with super-detailed belt of '12 Apostles'. Most contemporary engravings show a looped carrying strap attached to the gun-rest just below the fork. We have left off the canteen, knife and haversack, for reasons given in the text; if you like you can scratch-build a 'snapsack', usually a large, shapeless bag slung round the body and hanging on the back.

The English Civil War

One of many slightly differing patterns of musketeer's cartridge belts. Note how the wooden canisters are arranged on strings held together by rings. Immediately left of the bullet bag is a powder flask, carved as a larger version of the individual charge canisters.

plain cuffs and bare hands. Don't forget to add a 'slow match' to the musket and left hand, out of thread—the coloured illustration on the kit instructions shows the arrangement. A loop of thread or stretched sprue can be added to the rest—see photo.

And now, the slung equipment—a nightmare for those of you who have a rigid conscience in such matters! The sword, bullet bag and powder flask should be slung on the baldrics, as in the instructions. We suggest you omit the waistbelt, the water canteen, the haversack and the knife together. The canteen is definitely unconvincing for the mid-17th Century, when all such refinements were personally provided. A leather bottle, or a pottery or wooden flask, would be feasible; but this regulation-looking canteen, while passable on a single figure, would look most unconvincing on each member of a group of musketeers. The knife is also pretty unlikely—again, you could get away with it on a single figure, but this would be a private item, varying enormously in size and method of carriage, and this neat bayonet-shape would look out of place on more than one man in any group. The haversack looks far too neat and Napoleonic—again, men would bring their own pouches, wallets, or bags, and this moulding looks far too 'regimental'. Having disposed of these, there is no reason for the waistbelt, so omit that as well. Finally, the dread saga of the Twelve Apostles. . . .

The kit assembly instructions show these as being cemented directly to the figure's crossbelt whereas, as the pack front illustration shows, each was, in fact, suspended from two little strings. These were to allow enough 'play' for the musketeer to handle the cartridge while he loaded his weapon, sliding the belt around his body to bring full cartridges to the front each time. Difficult to represent—but in our readers' interests there is nothing we will not attempt! Gerry paled, gulped and then sat down to destroy his eyesight, nerves and temper by making two minute lengths of stretched sprue for each cartridge, and cementing them to the cartridges, and each end to the crossbelt . . . his sufferings were too ghastly to relate. The sprue is so fine it snaps at a touch (Gerry swears it broke when he *breathed* on it) and melts away to nothing at the merest hint of cement. Placing each end accurately is a task best suited to a highly trained spider, rather than a normal human being. But it *can* be done, and in the interests of authenticity should certainly be attempted. Marginally easier, but more difficult to paint, would be tiny lengths of fine nylon thread. Fuse wire of the finest grade is easier to handle, but harder to cement. Take your pick. In any case, we strongly recommend that these small items of equipment be painted before assembly—something we did not think of at the time, to the acute distress of our stalwart editor, who actually painted the figures!

Modelling Civil War figures

The pikeman

Again, this kit makes up into a sturdy and attractive figure, given minor adjustment. We generally followed the sequence in the kit instructions, but again, take care when placing the head and collar—it is much easier to arrange the slung equipment if you leave head and collar until after the belts are in place, so that the collar can 'fall over' them where they cross the shoulder. When joining the two halves of the torso, use your favourite filler or 'soup' to smooth over the join lines in the shoulder straps of the cuirass, and the coat skirts, but *not* the edges of the front and back plates down the ribs—these were two separate plates and had a pronounced join. Trim and join the legs to each other, and to the torso in the usual way. When cementing the tassets in place, make sure they fit snugly to the body along the top edge, but they can stand proud all round the other edges—they were in fact fixed to the breast plate with straps.

After dealing with the slung equipment, assemble and add the head, helmet, and collar. The modeller wishing to build up a squad of pikemen for a diorama can ring the changes by substituting one or two of the superbly individual heads from one of the Multipose kits—8th Army, German Infantry, Afrika Korps or US Marines. Cut these flat to take the helmet at the correct angle and height; add collar from plastic card softened with liquid cement or 'soup', and hair from putty. It would not be unconvincing to omit the helmet on one or two figures; you could make from putty a woollen Monmouth cap—like a World War 2 'cap comforter', perhaps with the long 'tail' folded over and tucked into the 'turn-up' at one side. You could also give a pikeman a slouch hat, from another kit or made as described under the musketeer. Even the barred 'pot' helmet from the mounted kit would not be out of place, particularly for an officer. When adding the plumes to either of the two kinds of helmet, we suggest you ring the changes—especially if more than one figure is to appear together. Add more fine grooves to the moulded plumes with a knife-point; make your own plumes from putty, suitably detailed; or use trimmings of actual feathers, 'furry' string or hair, cemented into place. Helmet chin-thongs can be added if you like.

Much the same applies to the slung equipment as to that of the musketeer. We dislike the uniform appearance of the haversack, canteen and knife, and suggest you discard some or all of them. The sword would more typically be slung on a baldric. Make one from plastic card, of a width to suit the section of sling moulded on to the sword scabbard, and sling it round his right shoulder. We suggest using the big buckle provided for the waistbelt on this. Add the waistbelt as per the instructions—it nicely represents the narrow strap which joined front and back cuirass plates together at the waist—and use either a little Historex buckle from the spares box, or a painted or scratch-built substitute. Again, 'offer up' your chosen arms and pike to the torso to check the position and fit before cementing. You could add a sash round the waist if you liked: cut a wide strip of thinnest plastic card, soften with liquid cement or 'soup', fold over edges and corrugate surface to suggest folds, and stick to the torso. Tidy up with a knife, file and 'soup', and add bow and hanging ends from the mounted figure kit. Note, however, that sashes were typically tied *over* crossbelts.

The cavalryman

This is a nice figure, and we won't waste space by going through the sequence of assembly step by step, but will merely mention one or two tricky points which we discovered the hard way.

It is obviously very important to see that the two halves of the horse fit neatly with no visible join-line—on cloth or metal you can get away with a slight line, but no horse we've ever seen has a seam down his back and belly! 'Offer up' the halves carefully; file and fill with 'soup' or putty with great patience and care. When adding head to neck we found it best to trim the moulded bridle jaw-strap right off the head moulding;

fiddle till head and neck fit as neatly as possible, file and fill the join, then add a new strap from plastic card.

The fit of the two halves of the saddle, the back of the nag and the pelvis and legs of the rider is frankly bad on the example we built. The saddle, if joined together in isolation, won't fit snug to the horse; if you force both halves on to the horse before the glue sets then the saddle skirts stick out at an unlikely angle, and the rider won't fit on to it properly. The saddle is probably the best part to submit to radical surgery or softening with a solvent — the rider, thank God, covers a multitude of sins.

The rider should have rather prominent shoulder straps joining the halves of the cuirass — these can be added from plastic card. When ringing the changes, try filing off the fancy lace collar and adding a plain one from putty or card, for a common trooper. You could use different faces, from either of the foot soldier kits or from Multipose spares. Remember that *both* sides wore slouch hats and 'lobster-tail pots'; and remember that in any group the slouch hats would appear widely different, so use the alternatives already described. It's a pity that Airfix's superb little pistol isn't a wheel-lock, more typical of the period. Experienced modellers with a decent pictorial reference can make themselves 'scratch' wheel-locks, using the basic moulding provided and little bits of scrap and sprue. Pistols with rather longer and less markedly curved butts would also be typical — again, pretty easy to make for yourself. One of our conversions (below) describes a carbine of the day, which could be added to the mounted figure just as easily. If modelling a trooper, such details as the rather fancy saddlecloth and the skirts of the coat should be modified to a plainer appearance. With judicious filing and 'offering up', the peak and face-cage of the 'lobster-tail pot' can be cemented in the 'up' position, for a rider not actually in battle — these were a single assembly which often swivelled round the rivets fixing each end of the peak to the sides of the skull. In this case a thread or sprue knot of chin-thongs would be realistic.

By mixing the components of the three kits, changing poses with arms and heads from the spares box, scratch-building different headgear and weapons, you can produce a wide range of different Civil War soldiery. Although the variations on the theme of the mounted man are rather strictly limited by his pose, an action figure could be produced by using another horse and a fairly radically modified rider. Two easier conversions are described briefly as follows, and illustrated in the photos.

Dismounted cavalryman, or infantry officer

We made this fellow by marrying a pikeman's legs with a modified pikeman's torso and cavalryman's head and arms. The tassets are omitted and the location holes filled. From the bottom of the cuirass to mid-thigh, add the skirts of a buff coat from thin plastic card — its stiffness will give a good impression of the thick leather. Make a baldric from plastic card, and pass it round the body over the right shoulder, adding the sword scabbard (with hilt cut off!) to the left hip. Add a waist sash, as described above, covering the join of cuirass and coat, and with the bow and hanging ends from the cavalryman kit hiding any rough patches where baldric and scabbard meet. Add the gauntleted arms of the cavalryman, if necessary with hands chopped off and re-positioned at the wrist. Add either the pikeman's plain collar or a lacy one from the cavalry kit, and the 'lobster-tail pot' with peak and cage either up or down. As a variation, if he is to be a cavalry-man, you might try the bridle-gauntlet. This smooth iron guard covered the left forearm. Sometimes it extended in a sort of 'scoop' behind the elbow, so that the elbow was protected in both straight and bent positions. Sometimes it ended in a straight line just below the elbow, with a strap and button fastening to the sleeve of the buff coat. The accompanying sketch shows a simple pattern for making one from plastic card. The hand protruding below it should be very carefully carved, filed and painted from a bulky gloved-hand moulding, to

Dismounted cavalryman, or infantry officer. If finishing the figure as the latter it would be accurate and attractive to add a bit of finery—plumes and/or some modest gilding on the helmet, fringes on the gauntlets, etc. You could paint the sleeves any colour—red, blue, green, white, black or yellow—with rings of metallic lace, a line of lace up the front seam, and buttons on the vertical lace. The sash could be painted, as here, with a silver or gold fringed end, and the breeches could have a line of lace and buttons up the outsides. Stockings would normally be white.

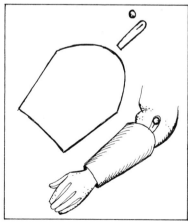

produce the flat planes on back and fingers, divided by scored lines, necessary to suggest a laminated steel glove with leather palms. The very experienced might like to try enhancing this effect by cementing tiny slips of plastic card to the back of the hand.

One variation, for a dismounted cavalryman, would be the big 'bucket-topped boots'. These can simply be taken from the mounted figure kit if you

A simple pattern for making a bridle gauntlet from plasticard. Experts can super-detail this by carving the hand to resemble a laminated iron glove, giving the gauntlet a turned upper rim, etc.

The English Civil War

arrange your figure in a mobile pose (see next conversion); otherwise you are going to have to do a great deal of cutting, re-positioning and filling and building with putty.

Dismounted cavalryman with carbine

This conversion is shown almost complete, on the base for its eventual mini-diorama. The pose is explained by our plan to build a section of stone wall, with a gate which the trooper is pushing open on some furtive errand; we haven't quite decided what he is creeping up on yet—chickens, or an unwary tavern-wench. . . .

Take the mounted man's legs, cut off the locating peg, and cement them together in a 'walking' pose. This is a matter of careful trimming, 'offering up' and filling until the correct stance is achieved. File the top of the new and untidy pelvis flat enough to cement the mounted man's torso in place. File and fill; then cover your accumulated sins

Dismounted cavalryman on the prowl, with plastic card buff coat and carbine carved from Baker rifle. The reason for the rather furtive pose is described in the text—obviously the details of the pose are up to you.

Half-completed conversion of the pikeman to produce the characteristic 'Order your pikes' stance of a body of foot prepared to receive the enemy's charge. Since contemporary regiments were usually of mixed pike and muskets, a small diorama could incorporate both the Airfix foot soldier kits in the same coloured coats and breeches.

with the skirts of a buff coat, from plastic card. Select and position arms of your choice, if necessary cutting and re-positioning the hands at the wrist, adding or removing gauntlet cuffs, etc. Add a baldric and the scabbarded sword; on our model we haven't yet added a nice big buckle and a loose end of strap to the chest. Add a carbine sling from plastic card, with the suspension hook from that of a Napoleonic cavalry figure kit. Add a collar—we used a lace one—and the head and headgear of your choice. We used an 8th Army head and a slouch hat, with putty hair. The brim was a disc of plastic card scored out with a pair of dividers, cemented on the flat of the head. A crown can be taken from the musketeer or Royalist cavalry head parts, or made of putty, or a cut-down Napoleonic shako; be careful to stick it truly central over the head. When it is firm, soften the brim with sparing applications of liquid cement and push it into position. A reasonable facsimile of a 17th Century carbine can be carved from a Baker rifle; cut the barrel off square at the ramrod pipe, remove the rear scroll from the trigger-guard, and carve and shorten the butt into the angular, rather dramatically 'scooped' shape of the period. Cement a tiny ring (from spare harness fittings) on the left side of the lock, and fix the sling's snap-hook 'through' the ring by cutting one of the them. The lock will do at this scale—flintlocks were in fairly wide use. A thread 'cord' can sling a powder flask round the body on the right side.

Pikeman at the 'Order'

We illustrate a tricky but rewarding conversion at the half-way stage; the basic anatomy work is complete and it only remains to add the head and the details.

It's a shame that, despite showing the pose in their coloured illustration on the instruction card, Airfix provide no parts for completing the pikeman in the most typical action pose—leaning forward with pike braced against the foot and sword drawn. The essentials are as follows:

Take the pikeman's right leg, and cut it through at ankle and kneeband. Re-cement, twisting calf and foot outwards until foot is almost at 90° to original front line of thigh. Take the left kneeling leg of a 95th Rifleman kit, and cut just below the knee; trim to match bulk, folds, etc, in right leg. Cut the pikeman's left leg immediately above the kneeband and cement to 95th thigh and knee. Join the two legs at the crutch, positioning carefully to match pose shown on instruction card; fill with putty and file to provide a convincing backside! Add rear skirt of buff coat from putty, card or carved scrap. Add pikeman's torso. Add tassets, re-membering they were fixed only to the edge of the cuirass. Add arms of choice—we used a couple of spares from Napoleonic kits, finding that the left arm of the French Line Infantryman in the ramming position was convenient for the bent, braced pike-arm. From this point on, file, fill, detail and finish to personal taste.

appendix

Information

First, a short list of some of the books relating to the Civil War which are in print at the time of writing.

Adair, John: *Cheriton* (Roundwood Press).

Ashley, M: *The English Civil War, A Concise History* (Thames & Hudson).

Clarendon, Earl of: *History of the Rebellion and Civil Wars* (Contemporary, edited W.D. Macray, OUP).

Cruso, John: *Militarie Instructions for the Cavallrie* (original 1632, this edition edited P. Young, Roundwood Press).

Featherstone, D.F: *Wargaming through the Ages, 1500-1792* (Stanley Paul).

Firth, C.H: *Cromwell's Army* (Methuen).

Gush, G.R.P: *Renaissance Armies* (Patrick Stephens).

Holmes, C: *The Eastern Association in the Civil War* (CUP).

Holmes, R., and Young, P: *The English Civil War* (Methuen).

Potter, R., and Embleton, G: *The English Civil War* (Almark, illustrated).

Toynbee, Margaret, and Young, P: *Cropredy Bridge* (Roundwood Press).

Wedgewood, C.V: *The King's War* (Collins).

Wenham, P: *The Great and Close Siege of York* (Roundwood Press).

Wesencraft, C: *With Pike and Musket* (The Elmfield Press; battles of the Pike and Shot period for the wargamer).

Williams, R: *Montrose, Cavalier in Mourning* (Barrie & Jenkins).

Woolrych, A: *Battles of the English Civil War* (Batsford).

Young, P: *The English Civil War Armies*

(Osprey, illustrated); *Marston Moor* (Roundwood Press); *Edgehill* (Roundwood Press); and Emberton, W: *The Cavalier Army* (Allen & Unwin).

Secondly, some wargames rules available for this period:

Wargames Rules, 16th and Early 17th Century, by G. Gush. Wargames Research Group, 75 Ardingly Drive, Goring-by-Sea, Sussex. Fairly complex.

Tercio Rules, by P. Harris. Tabletop Games, 92 Acton Road, Arnold, Nottingham. Very complex.

Birmingham 1500-1660 Rules, by D. Millward. Available from Skytrex, 39, Ashby Road, Loughborough, Leics. Fairly complex.

Musketeer Rules, by D. Millward, 259 Hinkley Road, Nuneaton. Complex.

Bayonet Rules. Available from Navwar, 48 East View, Barnet, Herts. Very simple.

Pike and Shot. English Civil War Rules, by D. Featherstone, 69 Hill Lane, Southampton. Simple.

15 mm Rules (the WRG set and some of the others above are designed for 15 mm as well as 25 mm figures). Peter Manning, 9 Athelstan Road, Bitterne, Southampton. Simple.

Wargames Rules for the Period 1500-1650, by Dave Nutt, 96, Birley Rise Road, Birley Carr, Sheffield. Fairly complex.

The Treasurer of the Pike and Shot Society (mentioned earlier) is P. Robinson, 27 Gorsdale, Sutton Park, Hull.

Finally, should the reader wish to discover a little more about what it was like to 'trail a pike', or simply fancy himself in the role of grim Ironside or dashing Cavalier, there are those for whom the Civil War is still raging nearly every summer weekend, and he will no doubt find a welcome in the ranks of:

The Sealed Knot. Lieutenant-Colonel Hastings Read, FH, 101 Graham Road, Great Malvern, Worcs.

The Roundhead Association. Lieutenant-Colonel A.A. Merchant, RA, 5 Beebee Road, Wednesbury, West Midlands.